My Father's Shadow

a memoir of faith, adventure, and healing from sexual abuse

CR

Kara Rodriguez

The events in this book are described based on the author's personal experience. Names, identifying details, and locations have been changed to protect the privacy of the individuals involved.

2017 Harriet Books Trade Paperback 2nd Edition
The publisher disclaims all liability in connection with the use of this book. Except as permitted under U.S. Copyright Law, no part of this publication may be reproduced, distributed, or transmitted in any form or by any means, or stored in a database or retrieval system, without the prior written permission of the publisher. All rights reserved.

My Father's Shadow © 2014 by Kara Rodriguez
Unless otherwise noted, Scripture quotations are taken from the Holy Bible, New International Version®. Copyright ©1973, 1978, 1984 Biblica. Used by permission of Zondervan. All rights reserved.

All Scripture quotations marked NLT are taken from the Holy Bible, New Living Translation, copyright 1996, 2004. Used by permission of Tyndale House Publishers, Inc., Wheaton, Illinois 60189. All rights reserved.

All Scripture quotations marked NRSV are taken from the New Revised Standard Version Bible, copyright 1989, Division of Christian Education of the National Council of the Churches of Christ in the United States of America. Used by permission. All rights reserved.

ISBN-13 978-0615940809
ISBN-10: 0615940803

Printed in the United States of America.

www.kararodriguez.com

To my father:
May you one day know Jesus
and accept all that He has to offer.

Contents

Preface i
Introduction 1
Broken 7
Betrayed 21
Unseen 39
Burdened 55
Confronted 61
Unbound 77
Entangled 101
Challenged 111
Triggered 129
Wedded 139
Entrenched 145
Encouraged 157

Preface

I'VE SPENT A GREAT DEAL of time and energy trying to make sense out of my reality. I've seen something like 15 therapists over the last 15 years. I've referred to blogs, read the books. I'm grateful for the research that's been compiled and knowing that I'm not alone has helped, but only occasionally have I uncovered words that truly address the gravity, the devastation, and my heart. In my search, I can't deny that I've longed for more.

I once read a short story about a woman who'd endured sexual abuse as a child and met Jesus as an adult. The account went sort of like this: "Hi. This is what happened to me. Then one day I met Jesus, and everything changed." Poof. Just like that? I mean, this woman was wonderful for having shared. It takes a strong heart to admit the damage that has transpired, and I do agree that Jesus is the answer. But when I read this, I couldn't wrap my head around what appeared to be another instantaneous deliverance story.

I've longed for someone to tell me about the war within her. I've wanted a woman to tell me about what happened to her, about the days she failed and the days she struggled to believe she deserved to be well again. I've desperately needed someone to tell me just how difficult it had been for her to arrive at such an admirable place, to tell me of her own struggles with sin. I've ached to hear someone tell me I was normal and that what I was feeling was okay. Not a practiced phrase, a verse, or a rehearsed recipe. I've needed the kind of empathy and vulnerability that can only spill out of someone who *really* knows. I've hungered for a woman to be real with me. And given the chance, I would've challenged someone to tell me everything.

That's why I'm here. What I needed more than anything when I was trying to piece my life back together was someone who was willing to dive into the deep. I'm here to tell you the truth, to assure you that change isn't going to happen overnight, to encourage you in your search for freedom, and to tell you the whole story.

This book is risky, and I feel the full weight of that risk. The thought of telling you everything has me hunched over and heaving huge breaths like I just got punched in the stomach. I don't hesitate to tell you that many times I've taken three steps backward only to move one lonely step forward. I will completely expose myself in the remaining pages. My history is blunt, and my sins are bare.

I don't believe that hiding anything from you will benefit you in any way because the rich redemption stories of the Bible are authentic and raw and not always pretty, but God tells them anyway. Woven in between God's perfection is humanity's imperfection, and the Bible openly describes the many stains of sin. At no point do I overlook or blatantly tolerate my sin. On the contrary, I share my struggles as a testimony to the wicked amount of pain I experienced as I attempted with all my child power to deal with the effects of the abuse.

I can only hope that by reading this story, you might walk away feeling a little bit bigger than the dark shadows within your life—the dark overtones of sin, pain, and rejection.

This is My Story

They stare at me from across the room
Faces, eyes
They wait and watch me as I breathe
Gasps, sighs

I don't have many positive childhood memories
Because of this I used to pause
Not knowing where to start
When preparing to share my story

I used to begin with a warning
Of the serious air about to filter in
I don't do that anymore, I can't stand it
I'd much rather speak openly about sin

I was first sexually abused around the age of five
I know my age because I recall what I was wearing
And I remember saying goodbye
To the piece of me that had died

I willingly suppressed everything
For the sake of holding my family together
On the inside, heavy
On the outside, light as a feather

Though shy and filled with shame
I was still basically a "normal" kid
I loved catching frogs, hunting bugs, and getting dirty
Just as the other tomboys did

I had an adventurous spirit
Even as a young one
Was in gymnastics even though I knew I was "heavy"
And coach seemed happy when her work with me was done

I had normal crushes on boys
And normal sad days
But when something else with my father happened
My normal would never be the same

I had no choice but to share my secret with the world
Thereby thrusting myself into adulthood at the age of 12
I was all grown up
But somehow nothing more than a little girl

I mourned and grieved
The loss of my father
Then I resumed living, stopped caring
Wasn't sure why I should bother

I stayed in Stevens Point
During the summer when I was 13
I started preparing for college
And maybe even began to dream

I kept typed pages
Of the things my father had missed
Thinking one day I'd be reunited with him
And I'd share with him my little list

In time, I stopped keeping track
I somehow knew I wouldn't see him again
I knew he wasn't coming back

I loved the beginning of high school, the beginning of dating
The beginning of sports, the beginning of belonging
But things quickly went south
From track to the dance team
More beautiful I thought I was becoming

From boyfriends
To pointless promiscuity
From friends
To drinking buddies and cruelty

From masked sadness to obvious hurt
From knowing God a little bit
To not even acknowledging His name
And relishing in the dirt

I continued living like this
For quite some time
I hid my shame and hurt with good grades
And performance and hidden crimes

It worked for a little while
I gleaned what I could from the approving comments
Covered up my actions with charm and a warm smile

Applying for college also provided hope
Off to Minneapolis
I felt the fleeting freedom that came with
Leaving home and starting a new
And doing whatever the heck I wanted to

I drank and partied
And met many friends

I aced most of my classes without studying
I felt free! But I surely didn't feel cleansed

Things changed though when I decided
To leave the "love of my life" because he wouldn't stop
Controlling and hurting me
I was sick of cleaning up his messes and taking care of him
I suppose I really wanted to start taking care of me

I moved out, left, quite literally tried to run
But my feet wouldn't take me as far as I wanted to go from him
I boarded a plane to Italy, then France
I relished in the sun and a new-found confidence

Yet I continued
To party
I continued
To bury

The following semester
I continued in my ways
Finding hope, security, value, and purpose
In my overnight stays

I'd run towards, then from
But again
My feet couldn't take me
As far as I'd wanted to go from them

I boarded a plan to Australia, then New Zealand
And this time the One I'd hid from
Followed me, met me there
He wouldn't leave me alone

God found me and Jesus comforted me
And within a week, I knew I was His own

A world turned upside down
I was zealous for love!
It wasn't in a bed, it wasn't in my head — yes, it was real!
Incredible, indescribable
Could've only been from above

Boys were friends
As they were in the first grade
Cares were gone
No, I wasn't afraid

I met God
At the intersection of "no worries" and grace
I couldn't have been more certain
I was in exactly the right place

I eagerly pursued God
Just as He was pursuing me
This time I wasn't running
I boarded that next plane to New Zealand out of freedom

But I soon
Slipped away
Dated one who didn't believe and reverted
To how I'd done life in the other days

The difference was this time I knew what I was missing
I knew what I was trading in
I boarded a plane to run
I knew I couldn't have both, so I left God and chose him

The fairy tale was for real
But it didn't include God
I was "living the life of a Christian"
But deep down I knew I was a fraud

Circumstances were wonderful, even perfect
Snowboarding, biking, beaches, and glaciers
But what looked like bliss wasn't
There was a giant disconnect

I poured into school
And finding somewhere to fit in
Unfortunately, I didn't realize that Christians were
Just as capable of hurting me and succumbing to sin

The people who hurt me
Pointed me away
So I boarded another plane
And I continued to stray

I was running from everyone and everything
I didn't expect to find God in Canada
As much as I didn't expect
To find him in Australia

Much like before
God pursued me, showing up on the radio
I heard a song I needed to hear more than anything
It showed me something I had previously refused to see

Blubbering like a baby with my Bible in a bath tub
I read His Word, finally went back to Him
And acknowledged all the blood

I left the man I was seeing
And bumped into the one who'd one day be my husband
As friends, we ran, ate, laughed, and played
We fell in love, I even told him I wanted to marry him

Then I hesitantly
Boarded a plane
I left for Costa Rica, then Honduras
Not wanting anymore to play the runaway game

I read my Bible all the time
I prayed and let Him sweep me away
I fell back in love with Jesus
Before I celebrated my engagement day

I ran home after all that had happened there
Robbed in Honduras and fearful for my life
And maybe a little fearful that nobody really cared

As two in love Christians
We began to do life
I studied and applied for a job
And planned to be a wife

Twin Cities Marathon
Biomedical engineering
Bungy jumping and sky diving
My relationship with live was endearing

That May I graduated, got married, got a job
And boarded another plane
Either my life was crazy
Or I was the one starting to go insane

I ran with James
And started to know him
Then we came home
And reality sunk in

I pitied myself
I saw the pain, felt the shame
I started seeking therapy and drugs
And all I could think to obtain

Writing every day
I boarded another plane
Got stuck in a downward spiral where I listened to the lies
Took the drugs, but got lost along the way

Then I stayed in Minnesota
I didn't board a plane
My heart vomited through a pen
I even welcomed the rain

I began to share my story
I started not to care about how I look
I did marriage and life
And community and the like

I saw progress between our winter lodge trip #1
And boarding a plane and our winter lodge trip #2
And I meant it all the more when I said to James, "I love you."

A New Year's goal
Was to start EMDR therapy
Partly for the sake of hoping
To one day have a baby

I started digging deeper than ever
Kept on writing
Continued to use my pain as a lever

We boarded another plane
This time to Switzerland
We talked with Bittersweet
We said hello to Unity

As I kept on expanding
The space between us continued to shrink
I was terrified at the thought of having a boy
And now that boy is the most grace-filled link

To truth
And knowing that God has a plan
To hope
And trusting that a man can be a real man

Which brings me to today
Life is simple but so very complex
At least things are much less tender now
From one day to the next

Focusing on community
And a life lived for God's glory
The pain, the problems, the paradise, the promises
This isn't baggage, no, this is my story

Gasps
Sighs
Faces
Eyes

Introduction

*"All changes, even the most longed for, have their melancholy;
for what we leave behind us is a part of ourselves;
we must die to one life before we can enter another."*
– Anatole France

YOU MEET ME AT A place called Riverview Café in South Minneapolis. I arrive on time to the minute. The intersection is among my favorites, with an old-fashioned theater and a picturesque gardening store across the street. The lady behind the counter knows my name. You sneak a peek at the receipt and see that I tipped a dollar for a single tea bag. How generous! But what you don't know is that I would've given her less if it weren't for all the math, and Riverview is the only place this side of the Mississippi where I tip like that. Nostalgia and sentiments are to thank. I've come here hundreds of times to work on this very story over a tea or a beer, usually a beer. And if I'm going to be completely honest like I promised, I ordered a tea today only because you did. I'd much rather be enjoying a beer or two (is three too many?) if we're about to get into the gritty details of my past.

Sitting across from me, you observe me and quickly come up with a few more inferences: I'm seemingly beautiful. Maybe I just don't know it. I'm awfully smart, so I must be gifted or at least must have followed in someone else's grand footsteps. My husband loves me. I love him. If you didn't bother to ask, it'd appear that the setbacks we encounter are not unlike the standard difficulties experienced by most, if not all married couples. From the outside peering in, all the information you're gathering is misleading you to deem me normal, my life functional, and everything in my past beneficial.

I dare you. Don't comment on how amazing it is that I charmingly "have it all together." I do. Sort of. A quick judgment from the world would indicate that sure, I'm happy. But if you sit with me long enough, the truth will spew forth in bitterness. Sometimes, I'm happy only when I feel pretty. I've desired knowledge and all the schooling because it seemed to distract the world from shaming me. My marriage has been a means to discover how I truly perceive the world, my past, and myself. I've been everything but beautiful. My world's been wickedly distorted. My world has been one where the victim is the perpetrator and time magically heals all. My ruins reflect the many lies that have set up camp in my heart.

Many people search for fulfillment because the grass is always greener on the other side, but I was caught up in the search because I'd never gazed upon the exquisiteness of lush green. My world was made up of dry sand and cement. A humble glimpse at one leaf of life left me appreciating what I had instead of questioning what I did not. For the person who's never experienced the true beauty of purity, there's simply no room for comparison once it's finally found. The innocence that was discovered was water in a vast desert. For this person, for me, life is lived in pursuit of developing this new identity. Life is a pursuit of restoration. Life is a journey of figuring out what to do with eyes that have been opened.

For the person who is blessed to have suffered little disturbance in her upbringing, there is a temptation to overlook the grace of her childhood. She trusts without questioning, follows without dreading, and in many ways, remains pure without realizing how truly delicate she is. Beauty exists but seems to remain unacknowledged. To the woman who hasn't experienced much hurt: You are not normal, but you *are* fortunate. I'm horribly tempted to not like you. At times I'm jealous of you, of the effortlessness of your childhood, but I'd never wish that you wear my shoes or carry my bags.

Maybe I don't look like the type, but I used to dance. And today I danced on the old, wooden floors in my living room instead of on stage in front of a crowd of people. I started with leg lifts. Then I added spins. And even though I've only taken one pointe ballet class in my entire life, I finished by neatly lacing my shoes all the way up my legs, tying the cutest little bows at the top, and shuffling across the room. I felt beautiful even when I was just standing there on my toes. In fact, I knew I was. Then the throbbing insisted that I gently lower myself onto the floor. I still felt beautiful though, and I imagined Him smiling. I couldn't see beyond my tears. Maybe I'm not comparing myself to the magazines or dieting to the extreme anymore, but I still strain to comprehend God's adoration.

Please don't pity me. I hate that. Besides, beneath your sympathy, can you confess that you wish you knew how to dance or that you don't feel all that beautiful either sometimes? It's funny because who said I'm that great at dancing? I mean, I was *okay*, given what I was up against. Everyone else had been shoved into expensive dance classes before they could even walk, whereas my experience profile included the Macarena along with violently jumping up and down at middle school parties. And after trying out for the dance team in college, I put on my street clothes, sat there like I was someone's sister, and snuck out the back door before it was over. I didn't even make the first cut. And who said I'm beautiful? Nerd is the word. I can't seem to get past this obsession with my weight even though I know there's nothing to be concerned about. And by the world's standards, I'm becoming more and more unsightly every day. My hourglass is ticking like a clock.

I know all about jealousy and comparison. It's just like an allergy. I used to take in every detail around me, fully believing that the valuable information I was absorbing would somehow further me in the competition I was in. Every lovely and attractive feature I'd see would send a rush of insecurity through me. Like blisters or blotches that emerge to combat an aversion, my ugliness would surface. And before I knew it, my instincts would rush to the front line to protect me.

Most believers I meet were virgins when they got married. In secret, I fear God's favoritism of them over me. I spend time with friends who seem to pray more than I do. And when someone prays at the dinner table, I think about how we often forget to pray at home. And it's hard not to open my eyes, impatiently stare at the food, and scan the table for dessert. When I see what more I could be doing, I battle twinges of guilt.

Do you know what? When I typed the word "dessert," I almost forgot an "s," spelling the word "desert." It's funny that a desert would be on my mind, but I suppose it makes sense if you consider all I've been through. I guess that's me, always contemplating something, maybe a little too deep for the average person. But can you blame me? I guess I can't enjoy my dessert if I don't remember the desert from which I came. This whole pursuit of healing thing? It's about dancing even when I don't feel beautiful. It's about learning to be vulnerable even when I feel insecure. I can't make my past go away, nor can I reduce myself to my past. I can't downgrade my life to a single story, one of abuse. George Bernard Shaw has said, "People become attached to their burdens sometimes more than the burdens are attached to them." And maybe that was the catch all along. Letting go has nothing to do with ignoring, but everything to do with incorporating. Maybe my dancing in the desert is my dessert.[1] It took many desolate days for me to acknowledge the fruits of my desert. It took years of error and longing for me to become who I am today, but become I finally did. And becoming I still am.

A day at Torpy Park

Dancing at Torpy Park at age 3.
(photo credit: *The Lakeland Times*)

Broken

I had a dream my life would be
So different from this hell I'm living
So different now from what it seemed
Now life has killed the dream I dreamed.[2]

MY MEMORIES ARE SORT OF muddled. I remember being a flower girl at a wedding, which I should've forgotten by now. I rehearsed fearfully, walked carefully, and stood there ever so nervously. I was only three. I remember our house before the addition was completed. I was also three when I shared a room with my brother, cuddled with a rainbow-colored blanket, and adored the sheep skin rug at the end of my bed.

I recall sitting in my mother's car in the middle back seat as we drove home on icy, snow-covered, snake-like roads. As we came to the bottom of a hill, my mom muttered in a quiet panic, "Hold on, we're going to hit." I even remember spotting sparks out my window as we collided with the other car and time stood still. That's when I saw fear on my mother's face for the first time. I was only three. I remember driving home after my Ronald McDonald birthday party. I stared out the window as I rested next to a heap of presents. I was five.

That's when everything went dark.

I know. Many have reassured me that a watered-down memory is part of aging. But I'm talking about something deeper: A subconscious forgetting of very specific time frames. The human mind is astonishing. The human body is capable of provoking memory loss as a temporary or even permanent coping mechanism in the event of mental, physical, or emotional trauma. Amnesia of this origin can so intricately entangle itself into one's perception of reality that even the absence of pivotal childhood memories appears to be normal. One is forced to live in the shadow of the way she perceives the world perceives her. Denial can be so deceiving that it requires a jolt—a complete shock to one's world—to uncover the truth. Even so, some memories can remain lost forever.

I remember my fifth birthday but not my sixth, and it wasn't until I stumbled upon a picture of myself huddled around a cake with seven candles that I could faintly recall my seventh. I'm able to reminisce about being three, but I can barely remember seventh grade science. I even had to read about my freshman year of high school in and old, chicken-scratch journal before anything trickled back. I find it rather disturbing that I've blocked out so much of my childhood. Shortly after I got married, it occurred to me that if I didn't slow down, rewind, and force myself to regurgitate even the blotchiest timeline, I may never comprehend the gravity of what was done to me.

When I used to think of denial, I always thought that it meant one of three things: to completely refute an experience, to fail to acknowledge a certain situation, or to insist that the world is perfect when clearly it is not. It wasn't until I learned about the denial associated with assault victims that it hit me. By minimizing my pain and suffering and overlooking my ongoing brawl with lies, I was proclaiming the reign of denial in my life. So I decided to embark on an adventure, a little detour through my past. I decided to lie down in my bed, wide-eyed and restless, and attempt to remember everything that I possibly could. I barely blinked that night, and just as I had predicted, I learned that a distorted and incomplete timeline had been suppressed inside of me for quite some time. An eccentric collection of memories and emotions soon flooded my mind with absolutely no lucidity. If my heart could vomit, its chaotic contents might resemble this:

> *The first room that comes to mind is the bathroom, before we redecorated it and after. We repainted it after my dad left. I used to think I had an aversion to the peeling wallpaper, but the holes by the base of the floor are perhaps what truly upset me. My sister and I blasted Pink's album, Missundaztood, as we painted. We belted, "You can run me over with your 18-wheeler truck, and I won't give up." It was a strange kind of comfort.*
>
> *We used to go out for dinner as a family, attend car shows, and ride around in the old convertible. My dad was always fixing up old cars. I used to help haul wood in the fall, and in the spring, I'd hunt for Easter eggs in my beautiful, white Sunday dress, before everything happened.*
>
> *Sunday school, church mission trips, and our family trip to Florida. The fort in our backyard had an amazing swing set, I loved microwave dinners solely for the pocket of pudding. My uncle used to take us fishing. Dad used to play his guitar in the basement, my brother too. My brother and I used to be in a church band together. We used to walk the path to my grandma's house on Christmas Eve.*
>
> *I can't remember a day when the news wasn't on in our house. My dad loved to watch the news and drink beer. He once offered my brother and I sip. At something like six-years-old, I found the stuff to be nasty.*
>
> *My parents' room had a full-length mirror that I spent a bit of time in front of, and the adjacent hallway closet was stocked with games. My brother and I used to pretend to be*

Power Rangers. I was the always the blue one, seeing as I loved to wear this blue, flowered shirt and a blue mood ring. Mood rings change colors, but this one didn't. It always seemed to stay the same blue.

Dad played cards with me a few times, and he grudgingly attended one of my swim meets. He played volleyball with me one time. I remember exactly what I was wearing when he did — that yellow tank top and those pink pajama bottoms with moons on them. How could I forget?

My mom rocked me to sleep until I was much too old for it.

My mom used to babysit all the neighborhood kids. I loved being home with my mom after a half-day of kindergarten. I was allowed only half a can of soda when I was seven, and I played with ants in the backyard when I was six.

We used to make homemade pizzas and camp out in the living room on Friday nights. This was a rather significant event in our household, one we commonly referred to as "fun sleep." There was a night of fun sleep with my dad. Half awake, half asleep, in and out, waking up to a pillow over my head. I could faintly see through my semitransparent pillow case. I knew it was him, his hands so big, his knuckles so hairy. In fear, I commanded myself not to move, not to breathe. I pretended to be asleep. I never wanted to uncover what would happen if he knew I was awake.

I used to catch salamanders in the backyard, tadpoles and frogs at the lake, and everything else I could get my hands on. I once trapped a very large snake in a cardboard box. Not convinced on the size of this thing? The snake was in the process of downing a fat bull frog when I entered the scene. I also used to catch Dad smoking outside. He'd never admit to it, but I wasn't an idiot. I saw it.

My dad used to tell me I was the most beautiful girl in

the whole wide world. I can still feel the sting of him reciting those same words to my friend. He used to flirt with my friends. Used to walk in on me while I was changing. I still wasn't used to wearing a bra at the time. I'd scream and scream, but he wouldn't leave. He never would. My dad said no to just about everything until I finally convinced him to let me have a kitten for my fifth birthday. My first kitten died the night I took her home, but the pain I felt that night was nothing compared to the other pains that were taking place.

I told my friends what happened to me at a late-night, middle school event. We snuck into a dark hallway, hugged our knees to our chests, and pinned our backs against the wall. That was the first time I'd told anyone besides my mom. I was 12.

One day a police officer picked me up from school. As I sat in the front seat, he explained that he was taking me somewhere safe. I stared out the window. Time, the ground, my heart – it was all frozen. One time I hyperventilated in my mom's car out of fear of the dark or fear of my father, I couldn't tell you which one.

I felt safe for the first time at Grandpa and Grandma's house. We stayed there after visiting with the detective. I was so ashamed that I couldn't even look at him. I had to use pictures to describe what my dad did to me. Even pointing to the parts where he touched me was...disturbing. I don't remember if I ever truly described how my dad hurt me, but sharing what I did was comparable to birthing a porcupine. It was even worse than when I heard the word "divorce" for the first time.

My doctor scolded my eating habits and called me fat during a physical exam. I started criticizing my body in front of my mirror.

The horses lived in our backyard in the barn we built together. The first time I saddled up, the horse bolted. My heart raced along with him before I was finally bucked off, luckily landing in a fresh cushion of snow. We were forced to give them away when my dad left.

My brother and I visited our dad after he left, only to find him drinking alone. We brought him a pie because I felt sad that he was alone. Nothing says, "I forgive you, Dad. Please say you're sorry and come home," like a freshly baked pie.

We moved. We had to get away. The first time I ventured back to the old house after we moved, I couldn't stand the stale, musty smell. It was as if the house carried the burden of all that occurred there, its vile grief still dripping from the ceilings.

I remember drinking and stealing throughout high school, but I also remember reading my Bible at times. I'd pin my favorite verses to a bulletin board. I even made a list questions I was going to ask God someday: What are our jobs here on earth? Do animals talk but we just don't speak their language? (And my favorite) Let's say there's a planet with people who have no eyes. It's all they've ever known, and they get along fine without them. Then when they die, their gift is the gift of sight. When we die, do we gain something like eyes? And we can't possibly comprehend what it is, like trying to explain sight to the people on the planet with no eyes?

I once wrote a letter to Dad describing in detail everything he'd missed. I used to think that he cared, that he missed me, and that I'd see him again. But I started to lose track. I never sent the letter. The last time I saw him, I was 13, sitting across the table from him in the lawyer's office. I'd somehow missed his smell even though he reeked of cigarettes, even though I had to ask him to hug me. Growing up, he never brushed my hair away from my face or hugged me purely. No, his love for me was much worse.

Towards the end of high school, I had a few anorexic episodes, though I've only ever referred to these phases as periods of not eating. I remember that sinking sensation in my chest when I'd remember my most recent food mistake. I'd turn to my mirror several times a day just to be sure that my last meal didn't put me over the ugly threshold. I'd dabbled in just about every beauty regime, but counting calories was like an old friend that always delivered, always answered when I called.

I remember Italy, France, Australia, New Zealand, and meeting my husband, James. My great-grandma passed away when I was 8, my grandpa when I was 22. He was one of few men, if not the only one, I trusted growing up. I was so unsure of my father, I used to hide under my bed with the keys when I didn't want my mom to leave the house.

I remember when I realized that my dad wasn't only cheating on my mom. He was cheating on all of us. I was speechless when I found one of his porn magazines. She looked nothing like me. She was tall, skinny, and had a huge chest.

But most of all, I remember mourning the death of a dad who hadn't died.

That's it. That's everything I could list as I lay in my bed that night. I'd inadvertently forgotten so much, and even after a full brain dump, a comprehensive timeline was still out of the question. At first, it'd seemed I'd come up with a lengthy list on journal paper, and yet 20-some years fits on a few short, typed pages. I've learned to grieve the memories that I'll never reclaim along with the memories I cannot return. And if it weren't for a stack of about 15 journals—from the depths of teenage, hormonal desperation to the highs of traveling the world—the rest of this story would've also been lost forever.

According to Mayo Clinic, "A pedophile is an individual who fantasizes about, is sexually aroused by, or experiences sexual urges toward prepubescent children (generally less than thirteen years) for a period of at least six months." Some pedophiles act on these urges and do not perceive their actions as wrong.[3] The term "sex addict" is often used to describe one who has an atypically increased sex drive. According to WebMD, "Sex and the thought of sex tend to dominate the sex addict's thinking, making it difficult to work or engage in healthy personal relationships. Sex addicts engage in distorted thinking, often rationalizing and justifying their behavior and blaming others for problems. They generally deny they have a problem and make excuses for their actions."[4] This proliferation of denial and excuse making is often simply another technique used to deceive. Deceitfulness is intentionally concealing the truth. In other words, the act of lying. Likewise, manipulation largely includes deceitfulness and can be described as controlling an individual by artful, unfair, or sinister means especially to benefit one's self.[5]

Some perpetrators go as far as to play the victim role themselves, approaching each situation with a "woe is me" attitude. Now, imagine someone whose personality and character exhibits each one of the above-mentioned traits along with alcoholism, a nicotine addiction, and a charming, humorous temperament. Now, imagine that this person also embodies this:

> *"Imagine – if you can – not having a conscience, not at all, no feelings of guilt or remorse no matter what you do, no limiting sense of concern for the well-being of strangers, friends, or even family members. Imagine no struggles with shame, not a single one in your whole life, no matter what kind of selfish, lazy, harmful, or immoral action you had taken. And pretend that the concept of responsibility is unknown to you, except as a burden others seem to accept without question, like gullible fools. Now add to this strange fantasy the ability to conceal from other people that your psychological makeup is radically different from theirs. Since everyone simply assumes that conscience is universal among human beings, hiding the fact that you are conscience-free is nearly effortless. You are not held back from any of your desires by guilt or shame…The ice water in your veins is so bizarre, so completely outside of [others'] personal experience that they seldom even guess at your condition."*[6]

Can you fathom this person? I can. Sociopathic tendencies are a result of nature as well as nurture. The disorder typically ripens at a very young age. I can't be certain that this was one of his conditions, but the word has been used to describe his tendencies.

At dawn, this bird sings. But in the wicked world I grew up in, a robin wasn't a signal of hope or a sign that warmer days were to come. Robin was the name of the person depicted here. Robin was the name of my father.

To Rescue a Robin

*Fire. That's what his chest reminds me of.
Capable of hate. Capable of love?*

*Reddish and orange and seemingly warm.
What power is enclosed in his red little form.*

*The area around his heart part is inviting.
And his songs of affirmation are more than exciting.*

*Welcoming and alluring, his chest begs me to lie next to him.
Be close to his heart and all the love that's within.*

*But ice has just as much power to scald.
I feel that burn when a call isn't called.*

*Wait, I feel no heat all nestled up next to him.
I feel no heat, not even at the sight of him.*

*I long to extract every vice from within.
Use my warmth to insulate and to warm him.*

*But when I come near, he flies away.
He flies away and never stays.*

*Yet he brings much hope.
When I am in pain, he helps me to cope.*

*He understands when it's time to sing.
He delivers a glorious song every spring.*

*I don't fear his lovely singing.
The calls, the tunes, and all the ringing.*

Perhaps a new time has finally come!
But oh how I fear the song left unsung.

Each one higher in pitch, three short calls he makes.
The world and the forest he violently wakes.

Sometimes he neglects the pauses, singing glorious waves.
Our sounds echo, our chests empty caves.

If I close my eyes and let his sounds take me,
I succumb to the dream where heaven awaits me.

His sounds have wired me to perceive light before me,
Even if shadows are all I can see.

This morning. Out the window. I hear his voice.
I jump out of bed as if I have no choice.

I step outside. Allow myself to breathe.
That's when I see him, perched among the leaves.

Parked on a branch, continuing to call to me.
He knew his sounds would somehow summon me.

Parked on a branch, continuing to call to me.
A woman he continuously begs me to be.

Sometimes he hops, rather than flies,
But when he flies, I can see freedom in his eyes.

He sees me, all of me.
A woman he calls and begs me to be.

He takes from me. He always receives.
And there's no need to question just how much he believes.

That I am the prettiest girl in the whole wide world.
That I am his princess, all snuggled up and curled.

Next to him. I dance.
He takes off. I watch.

He is the cause. And I am an effect. He sings. I sing. He swoons,
sending my heart over the moon.

No! He spirals and heads straight for the glass.
He spirals and twirls and lands in the grass.

No. There's no way I can stop it.
I've only enough awareness to stand by and watch it.

The thud is piercing and painful in my ears.
All limp and numb, the embodiment of my fears.

I look down to the ground and see that brown belly facing up.
I fold my hands and quickly make a cup.

What on earth has he done?
And where is the light? Where is the sun?

I squat down, onto my knees.
I jump up when I see motion. I see that he still breathes.

I reach for him. I reach out to him, to hear him, to help him.
Why is the light becoming so dim?

His beak pierces my hand. A drop of blood falls to the ground.
Now I know I'm too close. Now he makes not a sound.

I reach. I swoop.
I nurture. I regroup.

I keep quiet of the things that I've seen.
I never frown, never slouch. On him I always lean.

For all that I fear is the song left unsung.
I no longer fear all the harm that's been done.

I stroke him, coax him.
I sing when he doesn't seem to listen.

I smile. I invite him.
I do all that I can to help him to sing again.

And when he does, he flies away.
And I can rest easy for one more day.

When I look up to the sky, I see him. I see sin.
He's perched on the highest branch as if I never saved him.

There's so much that I've gained, but it's everything that I've lost.
I wonder if I would've kept quiet if I truly knew the cost?

I've tried to rescue a robin. I've tried to save a father.
If I'd known he'd never love me, maybe I wouldn't have bothered.

But that was then. This is now.
I know I must release him. Some days I'm just not sure how.

But it looks like I don't have to, for he has flown away.
Has nothing to sing. He has nothing to say.

He's gone. He's left. He's never coming back.
And I'm left here with these memories to forever unpack.

Betrayed

> *"The opposite of love is not hate, it's indifference."*
> – Elie Wiesel

IN THE TWO WEEKS THAT followed my night of remembering, I constantly contemplated. I tried to evoke additional memories, but what I added to the list was minor: a field trip, details regarding shop class in middle school, and a few other arbitrary facts. Otherwise, most everything was, and still is, a blur.

But I guess the intensity of a couple of memories makes up for the vagueness that surrounds them. I recall nearly everything about the night when my dad first touched me. My mom and my brother were away for the night, so I begged my dad to hang out with me. Naturally, I assumed that he'd be up for the Friday night fun sleep tradition in light of their absence, but I had to plead with him before he agreed to spend the evening with me. A movie played for only a little while before he became anxious and switched the channel to the news.

In my disappointment, I arranged my blankets and laid myself down for bed. I faded in and out while I slept on the couch, disrupted by the television noise and the lights still on. In the foggy moments when I'd wake up, I'd toss and turn and ask my dad why he wasn't going to bed yet. I kept telling him I wanted to cuddle, to which he consistently replied, "Hold on. I'm almost done."

Dad continued to drink until the wee hours of the morning, downing an incomprehensible amount of alcohol. I woke up that night one more time, and when I did, I didn't fall back asleep. That wasn't an option. My clothes were being stripped from me. I was wearing my Seven Dwarfs night gown, which was an oversized, green dress of sorts. Over the years, I've realized that I couldn't have been older than seven the night it happened, but I was probably closer to five or six. A few years ago, I stumbled upon a picture of myself wearing the same green pajamas, about to make to wish. I counted seven candles on my cake.

A pillow was placed over my head. I never moved, flinched, or spoke. I only waited. I was afraid of what might've happened if he knew that I was awake.

It could've been five minutes. Or five hours. I don't know.

I felt ashamed. I felt fear, disgust, anger, and pain. There was a brief moment the following day when my heart burned in my throat as I considered saying something to my mom. I thought about telling her. I remember exactly where we were standing — in the archway to the living room. I remember just how awkward my parents' conversation was and how strange our interactions were. When my mom asked us how our night was, I froze at the thought of my father becoming angry at me, hurting me, my parents getting a divorce, or worse, losing what was most important to me: my father's love. In that moment, it was as if I instantly forgot everything. But of course, I didn't forget. I only buried it.

I became numb. Gray inside.

My dad didn't need to say anything. His silence spoke a great deal to me. Quiet coercion commanded my support. An inaudible instruction summoned me to protect him. A plea saw to it that I lived up to his desires, lest I forever live a life absent of love. It was a fearful, dreadful love that induced me to comply. I needed that love for simple survival. What's more, the fate of the family obviously rested on my shoulders. In not telling, I saved my family. I was the glue that held them together.

I opened my music box and tallied the ballerina's turns. Elegantly up on her toes, with a smile that never widened, a smile that never faded.

By the time I was seven, I was already much too old for a seven-year-old. I was all grown up seeing as sexual foreplay was no longer a mystery. My eyes had been opened. The world was dirty to me, and if I couldn't trust my dad, who could I trust? Life had become a series of guessing games and attempts to overlook what had happened.

When I was eight years old, I was already disgusted with my own body. I regretted having worn that belly baring shirt during our family trip Florida. I was much more comfortable on the swim team where I got to wear this one-piece swim suit that was admittedly difficult to breathe in, but it hugged my excess fat close to my body. During that trip, my dad had a certain look in eyes when he'd glance at me. I can't put a finger on it, but something clicked inside when I gazed back at him. I realized then that my dad *knew* something about me, about us. But what?

I began exerting most of my energy towards enhancing my appearance and sexuality at an early age. During the fifth grade, I was most jealous of a beautiful, skinny, auburn-haired girl. Most of the boys liked her, especially when she wore these cut-off jean shorts that showed her underwear when she sat down. I could see completely up her pants as I sat in my desk right across from her, and I'm sure the boys could too. I assumed I could learn from her, follow her lead. By words or action, she was always providing me with what I thought was critical advice: Never wear your hair in a ponytail with your hair parted. Shave your legs before they really need shaving. Bras are for pushing up, not holding down.

Our class once went on a picnic at a nearby lake. I spent hours the night before the picnic posing in front of my mirror in attempts to convince myself I that liked my body in a tankini. It worked. I concluded before bedtime that I looked cute. But that conclusion was destroyed when Miss Popular paraded to the class outing in her all-too-perfect string bikini that showed off her all-too-perfect body. She won the pie eating contest that day. I remember seeing frosting smudged all over her barely budding breasts. That was the day everyone confessed a crush on her.

I was making significant progress with one boy until he saw her without her clothes on. Why is it called a crush anyway? Is it because infatuation always leads to pain?

I was thrilled when I was invited to her house along with six of the most well-liked girls in our class. I'm convinced I was invited because I was that "friend of a friend" tag-along. But I didn't really care. I couldn't have been more excited that I'd been invited! Of course, I had to prepare, so I pleaded with my mom to take me to the store. Being accepted at the party meant that I needed a more fashionable sleeping bag and some new underwear. Ultimately, I was proud to wear the purple underwear I had picked out. They covered up what I considered to be my trouble areas and accentuated the parts that I liked about myself. Even at that age, I saw changing in front of other girls as a performance, one that would define my worth.

At the slumber party, the girls all ran around the house, which was ultimate chaos, all the prancing around the yard half-naked. They jumped into the snow and ran back to the hot tub again and again. I half-participated by lounging in the tub and observing their inexplicable confidence.

After many giggles, everyone felt comfortable dressing in front of one another, except me. I quickly changed under my towel. I hid my underwear in my bag. These girls were wearing bras. And one had on a thong. I'd never worn a bra before. I'd never even seen one on a girl my age. And a thong? What on earth was that? And what was its purpose? It seemed like a horrible idea to me, at least at the time.

It wasn't long before I heard whispering and hushing in the other room. Since I was the only girl not involved in the conversation, I logically assumed the group was laughing at my expense.

"Come on! Tell me what is so funny." I pleaded.

"No!" The group chimed in unison.

"Why not? It's obvious you're talking about me!" My begging proved to be successful as this was their response:

"You…" one girl started.

"…have…"

"…big…"

"…underwear," another finished.

Four girls stood in a circle. They each uttered one word in this humiliating sentence while chuckling, my friend included. Tears welled up as I tried to choke them back.

"Why don't you just call me fat?" I hissed. Then the girls scurried off as if they'd gotten what they'd wanted: victory over my dignity.

I knew I was bigger than most girls, and I hated that about myself. I used to spend a lot of time standing naked in front of my bedroom mirror. I analyzed my body. I examined my stomach. I even placed tissue under my shirt to make it look like I had boobs. I would scrunch up my clothes and attempt to picture what I'd look like in lingerie. Yep, at 11 years old I was already hard at work, crafting my sex appeal, doing all I could to measure up to some stupid "ideal."

I was too young, too naïve to realize that not eating food could've made me thinner. Otherwise, I would've developed an eating disorder a lot sooner. Somehow, I managed to maintain my love for food until my dad conveniently intervened one day. I was sitting on the couch eating potato chips for my nighttime snack when I heard him utter in the kitchen, "You shouldn't let her eat like that. It's going to keep making her fat."

Kara was the prettiest girl in the whole wide world. But this phrase was a distraction, a decoy, a momentary uttering, a swift glance in passing. To get what he wanted from me. Why else did he also call me fat?

I was the prettiest girl in the whole wide world, but not because of my big brown eyes or my long and enchanting braid. The saying was simply the form of enticement my father used to get what he wanted from me, what he needed from me. I was never a real princess, only a fraudulent replica of one for a time, like a doll that's used as currency to enter the land of make believe. And just like any doll, I became tattered and torn. Then I was tossed to the side.

"Are you kidding?" My mom snapped back in anger and disbelief, yet my dad overruled. He always did. This truth was verified when my snack was taken from me. I was fat. And by the time my doctor—someone guaranteed to speak the truth—told me to start eating one piece of pizza instead of four, I couldn't have been more certain that the words "beautiful" or "skinny" were never going to be used to describe me.

Eventually, I started to lose some of the weight. It wasn't due to a lack of eating though. It was the stress that caused my skin to cling to my bones, my pants to slip from my hips. Honestly, I never really considered anorexia until one of my teachers accused me of being anorexic.

The air clung to me on that humid day. The grass was freshly cut, sending out the sweet aroma of summer into the air. The sound of sawing suddenly stopped. My dad emerged from the garage, sawdust clinging to his sweat. When I was 12, I used to wear these goofy, fuzzy, pink pajamas with obnoxious purple moons on them. They were childish, but I liked them. I was wearing my cherished childhood pants and a spaghetti strap, yellow tank top when my dad heroically decided to play volleyball with me for the first time. I was ecstatic he wanted to spend time with me.

"Kare Bare," he called me. And "Kara is the prettiest girl in the whole wide world," he said.

There were a few times when I did believe him. This was one of them. When he said those words that day, I smiled. My eyes sparkled as if to say, "Thank you!" Oh how I was my daddy's little girl! I could see where I was heading, the wind at my back and a clear road up ahead.

After playing with my dad, I ran inside for a shower. I breathed in the sweet satisfaction of summer and having spent time with my dad. I was completely giddy, but when I stepped out of that shower, reality filled the room, fogged up the mirror, and I could no longer see myself. The muck-brown shower curtain. It'd been there for as long as I could remember, just like everything else in my family: There was love and typical imperfections.

I could faintly hear a drill, but I thought nothing of it. I was used to those kinds of noises because my dad was busy building our dream barn. I was hunched over, drying my long hair upside down like I'd always done when I saw something rapidly move out of the corner of my eye. At first, I thought it could've been a mouse that had wedged its way between the cracks in the floor, but it didn't take long for me to begin to compile the evidence. I screamed. My mom came running. She busted open the door in her worry.

All I managed to say was, "I saw something peeking out of that hole down there." My mom asked me what it looked like. I could still feel the sting of my father's beam of vision on me. He saw my hair. He saw that I was pudgy. He saw my outline.

But Dad, I don't see whatever you thought you saw in me.

"Get dressed quickly and meet me in your bedroom." My mom had already deciphered what had happened, whereas I still wanted to ignore the truth: My own dad had created a mechanism to spy on me in the shower.

"Tell me what happened," she pleaded.

"That's not all."

"Kara, tell me what happened."

"That's not all," was all I could say. I was in a ball on the floor with my head between my knees. And when I looked to the blue paint on the walls, I saw that it matched me.

I wailed on my bedroom floor well into the morning.

Mourning.

It was obvious I was utterly distraught over what had happened, but I was even more concerned about the memories that came flooding back, as if the "shower incident" was a match that had lit an entire forest on fire.

I remembered everything. Suddenly. All at once. I was a body unplugged from The Matrix, and there was no going back. I couldn't un-know it. I could no longer deny it.

"I need to go talk to your father now," my mom said.

"No, Mom. He'll hate me!"

"Kara, I need to."

My mom spoke with my dad in between consoling me. She acted as a mediator as I attempted to make sense of what was done to me. What was going on? And what was going to happen? I pressed my ear against the wall. I needed the comfort of my parents' voices. I heard a few mumbles, but none of it made any sense.

At first, my dad wouldn't even admit to it. But a few short hours later, my dad asked me, through my mom, to meet him outside at the swing. And with one small tear and an absent-hearted apology, I chose to forgive him.

Where was my brother? I didn't see him at all that night.

I wrote this much of my story when I was only 13 years old. I found the hand-written notebook pages when I was 26. Those same pages contained a transcription of the horrific newspaper article, the one about my father's daughter, every word.

Days passed. My bedroom walls' color shifted with the light from the sun, but my color stayed the same, the color of complete heartbreak, the color of shame. Weeks passed before I expressed to my mom all that happened to me when I was five.

Truth or dare.

Dare.

Mom asked me to tell some man what my father did to me.

But I chose dare. Not truth!

But the dare was to tell that man the truth, to tell myself the truth. When I went to open my mouth, the words wouldn't come out. My mouth was dry, my tongue ripped from me. My eyes strained. My eyes began to sweat out of confusion, not desperation.

I made not a sound when I cried, but my tears did when they slapped against the table in front of me. The first one landed: snap. The second: shot. I closed my eyes, and I saw a picture of that girl who was supposedly pretty.

Kara was the prettiest girl in the whole wide world.

The man that sat across from me asked me one more time to tell him. When I refused to speak, he left and returned with a stiff piece of paper in hand. With a slight hiss of friction, it slid across the table, begging me to point to the parts where he hurt me. I saw all the lines of her body, that faceless paper girl. She was only an outline, traces of her pieces.

That outline.

The flash of the camera was delayed, but it illuminated my hand as I pointed to the parts where he touched me.

I quickly became angry that my parents were inevitably going to get a divorce. Unfortunately, I directed that anger towards my mother who rightfully made the decision to leave my father. I wish I would've known then what I know now: My mom acting on my behalf would play a vital role in my healing.

I'm grateful for a mom who understood the impact that the abuse would have on my entire life. Shortly after the community learned of it, one attorney proposed that my father receive only probationary consequences. Because with only probationary penalties, my dad could still "be a father" to me and provide financial support. Continue being a father to me? Because he was so good at it? Thankfully, my mom fought back by telling them that probation would only minimize what was done to me. She told them that I needed to understand that what he did to me was wrong. Because without my father facing any consequences, I wouldn't get the healing I needed.

As an adult, I'm able to recognize that I had a pretty shitty father, but I was a kid. I was angry. I loved my dad and my naïve "reality." All I wanted was to forget about everything that had happened, but forgetting was going to be difficult to do with the abuse legally documented.

The battle was long and hard to ensure my father spent time in prison. I missed him before he was even gone, and it was difficult to let him go. My heart ached whenever I pictured him sitting alone in a prison cell. Sure, I was hurt, but I think I hurt even more for my dad.

Unexpectedly. Inexplicably. Something deep inside of me began to awaken to the truth. My dad wasn't coming back. I don't know how I knew, but I knew. I'd never see him again. My sorrow began with a great deal of torture, but it ended with me grieving the death of my dad.

I created a small scrapbook of my dad, something I could remember him by in the years to come. It included pictures of him cooking his concoctions, playing his guitar, cuddling with me as a baby, and being the goof that he'd always been. I hung onto it for 16 years, kept it tucked in the back of a bookcase, packed it into a box whenever I moved. But when I dedicated two weeks to a Japanese-style cleaning frenzy, I made a commitment to myself to rid my home of anything that didn't bring me joy. I discarded every picture of my father except for one and the entire scrapbook minus the last three pages.

In pink ink, I'd penned a poem about my dad. What age I'd acquired in my youth. The only way for me to attempt to carry on at the time was to believe with all my heart that God would use me to save my father. "I'm just lucky I've been able to continue everything I love, school and my friendships. By knowing that I'm helping my dad, I've been able to piece my life back together," I wrote.

Daddy

God, You must hate me
Why else would You choose me?
One thing after another shooting me down
Next thing I know
I'll wake up tomorrow and won't be able
To see
Yet with all this I can still realize
You let me dance in my moment of glory
To think that you could hate me
I really am sorry
You made me the top of my class
Made me a great friend
Maybe one day
My heart, you'll mend
To have faith like a small child
To believe and to know
You are the maker not the breaker
Later, in time, my wounds you will sew
Someone took so much from me
My calmness, strong faith
No longer feel pure
In this case, there are not many things
There are not many things that can cure
I know this now
You're not the one that's done this
It was someone else
Someone who I actually really miss
He's gone, he's left
Was never really there
Did this to me
Hurt me bad

Yet he doesn't seem to care
You can tell me all this
A million times more
And yes my heart will still be sore
I already know that
And no matter what you say
I still love him
To this very day
Even though where he is right now
Light into his heart is dim
I hope and pray
One day the sun will come out
And shine within him
Hey God!
This is where you come in
Although my feelings on this are sort of mixed
I have to face it
Someone needs you more
Whose mind and heart both need to be fixed
I should be at the head of the line
Not have to wait my turn
I've waited this long so patiently
I need You to do this for me in return
Stand beside him
For I can wait
Convince him to give his heart and soul to You
God, I hope we're not too late
So now I know
Why I was put in this place
So in heaven, one day, just maybe
I can see his newborn face

The abuse happened at a time when such issues were not

often spoken of in a tactful manner. The local newspaper printed an article about what was done to me. It was supposedly considered legal because the paper didn't use my name. They simply referred to me as my father's daughter, yet in small-town, northern Wisconsin anyone who read the paper would've known it was me.

My secret wasn't willingly offered up. It was stolen. It was used as a media sensation apart from my 12-year-old permission. My father's daughter couldn't get out of bed that day. I begged my mom to let me stay home. Everyone in town knew my dad. Everyone knew my secret. I pictured my classmates reading the article at breakfast. Parents putting their coffee down and pulling their kids aside. Telling them not to go near me or my house.

My dad didn't just disappear from my life suddenly. The process was quite drawn out. It was kind of like getting pricked with a needle repeatedly in attempt to locate a vein. Imagine this needle sticking process taking place for about a year with no rest. Initially, I didn't see him much. My mom saw to it that he was away from the house when I was getting ready for school. He'd wait across the street at the neighbor's house…next to the yard that I used to get paid to rake. That chickadee sweetly sang to me as I worked and ignored what was done to me.

I longed to be loved by my father. I ached to have everything restored to a perfect state. I believed for quite some time that this restoration would come. It never did. On my 26th birthday, I observed it as a holiday representing a significant milestone: I'd been away from my father just as long as I'd been with him.

After a couple of months, my dad was living in a house less than a mile down the road. Shortly thereafter, my sister invited us to spend the night at a hotel with her. I remember the moment right before I knew the truth in its entirety. As if life wasn't atrocious enough, we soon learned even more despicable things about that man that I used to call father.

He was a dangerous combination, seemed to be the perfect embodiment of wickedness, yet he was someone to run to, not from. He even claimed to have Jesus in his heart as he deceitfully concealed his true self. He appeared trustworthy and authentic. The magnetism of sex appeared to be the root of all evil in Dad's life. He was brilliant, intimidating, funny, manipulative, charming, coercive. But there was more.

There was a moment when my family was sitting together on the couches of that hotel room in silence waiting for her to formulate the words. I'll never forget the look on my sister's face as she pieced together the evidence and bravely told us all that she'd come to believe about our father. Was it true? At the time, it didn't matter. What mattered was that my brain had received another, even more terrifying stamp. The image of my father filled with rage, capable of killing became a permanent tattoo.

I hid in the hotel bathroom and ran the water. I was experiencing for the first time what it was like to bleed. I sat in the blood until the water turned cold. I was shamefully naked and embarrassed by the mechanisms within my own body. I carelessly soaked in my father's filth, my filth. I loathed myself. I loathed how God created me. Over and over I asked myself, "Will I ever stop bleeding?"

Who was my dad? And how could my experiences with him and my new awareness of his past formulate any kind of clarity?

Horror. Horror owned me. The dark was all it took for me hyperventilate under the weight of a panic attack. Did my dad unlock the paddock gate and release the horses that night? My mom had searched for them. She'd marched through the mounds of snow for hours. Thought she saw someone sprint across our yard. There's nothing quite like the burn that's brought on by the cold. I remember her submerging her feet in the bath water that night, to bring back the warmth. I remember how she winced and bit back her pain.

Unfortunately, this new reality presided over the truth that I once knew in Jesus. The anxiety was too much, so I consequently shut off my heart to the world and numbed my fear with self-loathing, alcohol, nicotine, and association with the kind of men I was convinced I deserved. After all that was done to me and all that I had experienced, I was certain that I was unattractive and all "used up." Judith Herman describes it like this:

"Daughters of seductive fathers thus learned that they had two choices...(to) remain their Daddy's little girl, bound in a flirtatious relationship whose sexual aspect was ever-present but never acknowledged, or...attempt to become independent women...and in the process risk their father's (and all men's) anger or rejection. They reached adulthood schooled in the complicated art of pleasing a man and knowing virtually nothing about how to please themselves."[7]

After meeting with four therapists back to back, I gave up on pretending to swallow the pills that would supposedly make me "better." And there you have it. These experiences, these memories, this is what prepared me for high school.

My past acted as a pimple that festered beneath my skin. Perhaps my past was unseen from the outside, but it was so sore and I felt ugly knowing that it would eventually surface. Like a teenage girl self-conscious about her barely noticeable acne, I assumed that everyone could see my past in its entirety just by looking at me.

Without a doubt, I became quite the overachiever. Grades were everything seeing as I wasn't the best gymnast, the fastest swimmer or, in my opinion, the prettiest little girl in school either. My dad was a liar. Kara was *not* the prettiest girl in the whole wide world.

My science teacher narrowed his eye brows and pierced his lips as he commanded, "Relax already," when I received an A- from him. He meant well, but his words stung. I wanted — no, I needed — him to approve of me. Likewise, when my math teacher pulled me aside after class to rebuke me for wearing a tight shirt, I instantly shut down. Like my science teacher, this one also called me by my last name. I was always reminded that my father defined me.

"Mendez, I see that you're wearing a tight shirt again. You really shouldn't do that," he said as he shook his head and walked away, not knowing what he was doing to me. I bolted to the bathroom and tugged on my shirt. I attempted to stretch it out enough so that it would be acceptable to him. These men didn't understand that their approval was some of the only reassurance and guidance I'd receive from men growing up. And this new reality — one of shame, fear, hopelessness, and loneliness — compelled me to begin a search. I began to search for the perfect man, an emotional replacement for the father I never really had.

Unseen

I WAS STAGGERED BY HOW quickly my freshman year of high school flew by. With the surrounding schools aggregated together, countless activities, and endless introductions to the new and unknown, I was overjoyed and exhausted. Volleyball had initially stolen my heart, but the enticement of trying out for the dance team was too tempting to turn down. I have nothing against dance teams, but it sort of felt like I traded in my dignity for the ability to flaunt myself in front of the entire school.

Admittedly, being a member of the team was intricate and bizarre. I adored dance. Dancing made me feel alive for all the right reasons and all the wrong reasons at the same time. I craved the rush of competitions and performances, yet our practices helped me get close to the football team. I loved moving my body graciously, yet being on the team allowed me to wear (a lot of) real makeup for the first time. It didn't take much to convince me that makeup was the secret to beauty. A teammate of mine simply said, "You should wear eye liner all the time. You look better with it on." I thanked her. I believed her.

My first year of high school was filled with swim team practice and track meets. I wanted the world to be bewildered when it saw how great I was and how far I'd come, but springtime delivered an injury. I fractured the top of my foot. Perhaps I'd pushed myself too hard. It wasn't the first time. It wouldn't be the last. The brokenness in my body was a direct reflection of the brokenness within my soul. Since I could no longer run, I devoted all my time to the dance team, practicing as much as I could with one foot. The team quickly became a place where self-adoration and being in the spotlight secured my identity.

I ended my final journal entry for the year by stating that I'd successfully completed the year without a male role model. I wrote it with confidence and a hint of I-don't-need-anyone, maybe also a small dash of fuck-you. I then proceeded to attempt to fill that overwhelming void with every boy that I could convince to date me.

Let me assure you, it wasn't always that way. The purity of my first kiss validates that. We were standing in a stairwell when he romantically swept my hair away from my face and brushed his lips against mine. He liked me for me and wasn't looking to win me over physically. Our first kiss swept me away, but afterwards my heart sunk. I said goodbye to him as soon as I realized that I was downright terrified to be treated well. I was convinced that he had me mistaken for someone else.

The bad ones, they stayed for a time but would always leave. And the nice ones, I came up with excuses not to see. Some told me they loved me. But they *all* told me I was pretty. At least at first.

The real pursuit started with Alan. He was different from the ones that followed. There was much more heartbreak to be had with Alan, seeing as I was also completely smitten with his family during our 15-year-old dating experience. At the end of it, I wasn't just losing a relationship. I was losing a substitute dad. Nothing was more satisfying to me than when his dad congratulated me on hitting a curve ball out of the park.

And when I attempted to remove myself from the clouds of teenage lust, I openly admitted to my diary how fulfilling it was to spend time with someone's dad. Neither the happiness nor the subsequent heartbreak had much to do with Alan.

Except for one time when we were eating lunch together, and Alan stared across the room. Blonde hair, thin, undeniably cute. You get the idea. He didn't even glance at me between bites. Even worse, his parents were with us, so I was forced to hide my discomfort and hold in my bitter remarks. I couldn't quite grasp why, but I didn't feel like eating. And I wouldn't let it go. I poked at the issue until the grizzly bear was up on its hind legs, dripping with drool and sneering.

That fight ended everything. Then I received a letter in the mail from Dumped Jealous Girls United requesting that I mail in my first membership payment. No more than two weeks later, Alan began dating someone else, confirming every critical thought I had about myself. Looking back, it wasn't me that pushed him away. It was definitely my jealousy. I needed him to confirm my worth. I needed assurance that a young boy (or anyone for that matter) simply couldn't give me.

I used to keep a list of affirmations, things like making the varsity dance team and learning how to drive. I also kept track of my flirtatious episodes, the winking, the eye contact, the smiles. The more attention I got, the more I seemed to need it. It'd only been three weeks since the breakup, and I'd already shifted my focus to three other boys, their names all on a single diary page.

That diary remained untouched for the four months that followed that entry. Gaps in my writing have never been a good sign. An interruption in my documentation has generally indicated tremendous sadness or shame, maybe both. I lost my virginity, spent the night with a different guy a week later, and landed a new boyfriend without writing anything. And almost without remembering anything. After I'd given in with the first, I figured my innocence was gone, forever irretrievable. Saving myself for someone didn't matter to me anymore. If my boyfriend liked me and I liked him, that was enough.

I'd decided to attend a party following one of my dance competitions. With endless alcohol and absent parents, I became drunk for the first time. I get it. I chose to drink. I even chose to let him touch me. But.

Out of respect for girls who are violently raped, I don't like using that word, but I know I was taken advantage of. I was an exceptionally drunk 16-year-old girl, wading through her own personal hell. I bawled to this boy the following morning, unable to comprehend how our actions didn't automatically certify us as boyfriend and girlfriend, if not soul mates. But to him the issue was simple. He was annoyed, like how an older sibling grows irritated when his inquisitive little sister won't pipe down already. I was just a notch in a belt, an easy one, and he publicly declared that at school the following day.

I stopped dead in my tracks at the sight of it. Every muscle in my body loosened along with my jaw, sending my stack of books and pencils onto the tile floor. I kicked them aside carelessly and leaned in to get a better look. That's when a few tears began to formulate but didn't come out. I couldn't let them. My blinks saw to it that my cry stayed inside. I peeled back the tape and rubbed the piece of paper between my fingers to be sure that what I was seeing was real. The once encouraging good luck sign on my locker reeked of indecency and inadequacy. Beneath "Swim hard!" I saw the hideous words that I already knew were true.

"You should shave your mustache. And your area." Only

he didn't write "area." Navigating if I really needed to shave or wax between my legs (and live up to the latest porn-star standard) added a very depressing and humiliating layer of complication to my overwhelming insecurity, as if I hadn't already been objectified enough.

A sketch accompanied the words that were daggers to me. My teeth clamped down harshly, not pausing to consider where they might land. When they released their grip on me, I licked the spot where they sunk in. Blood. I buried my face in the upper compartment of my locker and considered climbing inside.

I reached into my pocket. I pulled out a needle. I took out some thread. I tensed every muscle and clenched my jaw to bear the piercing pain that came with every suture, every loop. When I finished, I looked to my mirror and saw a doll with a smile stitched on so very precisely. No one would ever know. No one would ever see.

I began to rationalize my actions. Continuing with my ways was fine because you can't gain stains on an already blackened shirt. I had a low standard for becoming involved with someone: He had to at least pretend to like me. It didn't even matter if I liked *him*. I'd learn to. And on the off-chance I wasn't justifying what I was doing, I was straining with all my might to change.

I hated that people talked about me. I looked to anything and everything for consolation. I stressed over my choir solos. I aimed for an Ivy League college. And in the privacy of my journal, I designated an entire page to keeping track of how many days I could go without lying, drinking, stealing, or having sex: those tallies were nothing more than wedges between me and God.

I craved attention, and I was jealous of the girls who could trap it. I began keeping another list, one filled with hate. Each boy reminded me of the things I'd done, and every girl was a symbol of all the things I didn't have: brand name clothes, money, beauty. A dad.

I began flirting with yet another boy. Though at 18, I guess he was a man. We'd text back and forth for hours, but we'd never converse in person for a couple of reasons: For one, he knew that us hooking up was illegal. Two, I wasn't a real *person* to him. I was the robot behind his porn app.

I learned a lot from him. He taught me how to look like the women he'd seen in his movies. He told me how to dress. He taught me that waxing and shaving down there was a "thing." He gave me step-by-step instructions on how to touch myself. I wanted him to like me, so I did what I was told until I became numb to the guilt and cold to the disgrace of being considered an object. I guess I wanted to say no, except when I didn't.

I liked country when I was with that one, hip-hop with this one. But what about me? I became whoever they wanted me to be.

Then I made a commitment to myself: To never again give anyone the power to hurt me. I became trained in the art of burying my emotions, but then the popular jock that I was sure would never under any circumstance show interest in me casually slid by my locker and asked me to prom. I said, "Sure." I kept my cool. I thought it was confidence that I was gaining, but it was myself that I was losing.

The weeks leading up to the dance seemed like bliss. There was an exciting outing with my friend where we picked out a purse and jewelry for the big night. I had a rejuvenating spring date with my mom, biking in the sun. I even caught a frog that day, something I hadn't done since I was a little girl.

I fell. I took the risk and let myself be happy, even if the only thing that was making me happy was the idea of being with this guy.

As a sophomore attending the Junior Prom, I was completely overshadowed by the other dates. The dance itself was anticlimactic, seeing as we didn't dance together, which meant we also did not kiss. And the post-prom party? A war zone. I walked downstairs to discover my date's ex-girlfriend on top of him. But once again, the issue was simple: I was the only thing standing in the way of my date having sex (and it wasn't because I wasn't willing). To him, I was just a huge bummer. A big, fat, stinking bummer. I was no different than a curfew or a parent calling and checking up on him mid-makeout sesh.

I locked myself in the bathroom. A senior girl (most plausibly only concerned with the party getting busted) sat on the other side of the door and tried to talk me out of leaving the party. When I emerged, I plopped down at a table, eyes dry, a beer in each hand. I pondered that girl's long legs and thin figure as I ate some pizza. And to my surprise (this is where the real romance begins!), sitting right next to me was the plastered dude that Miss Long Legs had rejected. His name was Nick. We bonded over (raised many beers to) our pain. Our longings. We were both each other's, like, second or third choice.

I owned that rejection though. In my journal I wrote, "He never got anything from me, and he never will!" Nice.

In the middle of all this, no one would've guessed that I was also straining to write a letter to my dad. But I couldn't figure out if there was too much to say or simply not enough.

I hated what I did, but I still did it. More than one guy would ask me what kind of underwear I was wearing via text on a daily basis. The rumors destroyed me because they were true. I'd keep track of how many drinks I could down in a single night, as if it were a competition. I continued to struggle to fill the deep void in my soul, yet each attempt only left me more broken than the one before.

Nothing changed in the year that followed, nothing for the better anyway. Every day I believed a new lie, and every lie I believed consumed more and more of me. As I continued to rely on myself for relief, my confusion amplified. I began to knowingly walk into traps.

My skin crawled. I hallucinated. I panicked when he shut off the lights. I kept forgetting where I was and what I was doing. I didn't really want to stay, but at that point, I didn't really have a choice.

When my next boyfriend and I broke up, I held onto the moments when he'd told me that he loved me like they were little keys to recovery. But taking a step back helped me realize the effect he had on me. If I wasn't drinking, he was angry. And he had lengthy phone conversations with his friends (other girls). At the end of it, he kissed me, let go of my hand, and said, "There's someone else." Really, dipshit? I never would've guessed.

I vowed to never let him touch me again. I swore off drinking and all sexual activity for the millionth time. I also failed for the millionth time. I let him back in before he could even finish asking, but I guess the second time was different. The second time he ended it because he wanted to leave for college in freedom (be allowed to have sex with whomever he pleased).

During my perfect partner pursuit, I also dated Nick, my fellow reject. We were together for about a year. He took me to the fall dance. I remember analyzing every girl there and concluding that I'd never measure up. When Nick and I lined up in the cafeteria to have our pictures taken, I noticed that my poopy prom date and Miss Long Legs (back together again!) were standing directly ahead of us. She was dressed in the most extravagant, white gown. She looked like a bride, and she resembled all that I'd wanted to be and more: She was stunningly beautiful, though I never would've admitted to it at the time.

I could feel what Nick was thinking in that moment. He didn't need to say it. I knew he was wishing that he was with her instead of me. She was the one he'd wanted all along. She was the one who wasn't me. And in that moment, I tucked my feelings into a place where I could access them only if I opted to. Then I regained my composure so I could move on with the rest of the evening.

A few weeks later, our relationship became physical, but afterwards, he grew incredibly quiet. Then he confessed to me that he'd cheated on me. With Miss Long Legs. And there you have it. Another boy confirmed every disapproving assumption I had about myself.

I remember watching porn with some of my friends at the time. I aspired to impress and was willing to take extreme measures to do so. My friend and I would send suggestive pictures of ourselves to my ex-boyfriend to prove that he'd made a mistake in leaving me. I let the line slip further and further until I ultimately engaged in many of the things I'd seen.

In my mind, there was a never-ending story. It was a story that began long before I could articulate the words with my mouth, long before I was conscious that I was even thinking them. My story began with recommendations from the world and continued with influential suggestions from boys. And perhaps the most important person in my life saw to it that I also understood the stories he had to tell.

Kara was the prettiest girl in the whole wide world. But suddenly, I couldn't remember who it was who said those words to me. Was it him? Was it me? Or was it the girl on the screen? The ideas and movies and images stammered and stuttered over and over, creating for me more memories, more tragedies. Snapshots. Girl after girl. Screen after screen. Outline after outline. Scene after scene. I was just another outline. Nothing was inside of me.

I thought about going anywhere, doing anything. I inexplicably felt happy despite everything, despite everybody. Looking back, I think that's called joy. "Maybe it's God. I want to believe that so bad, but why would God let this happen to me? Why would He leave me like this? Why would He love me like this?" I wrote.

That was the last time that I wrote in that journal. Perhaps it's symbolic for my desire to start anew. After all, that was the first time I'd truly acknowledged God in years. But unfortunately, I continued to collapse under the weight of my sin for quite some time. I failed to gain a true understanding of grace, and at the time pursuing God only made me feel worse about myself. I had it all backwards. Elements of faith began to evolve within me, yet I persistently placed my hope in relationships with men. I guess you could say I lived in their shadows.

I was certain I was dirty, but I was also determined to earn my importance through the means I was familiar with. No clothes. No courage. And no capacity for trust. That's who I was becoming.

There was one instance when I thought Paul might cry. I reached for his hand. Glass between us, I couldn't touch him. As he spoke to me over the phone, his voice crackled. We were both in prison, only you couldn't see mine.

After spewing forth assaults one night, I thought he was going to walk away, and maybe I'd be relieved of the burden. Then he asked me what I thought of the drinking, the drugs. And at even the slightest hint of consideration, I was lured back in. I loved him, I thought, but it was a naïve, "I've never truly been loved before" kind of love.

I thought I'd found someone special. I believed that in agreeing not to cheat, we'd uncovered the secret to making our relationship thrive. His loyalty wooed me, only because it was something I hadn't seen before. And someone was finally saying without hesitation the exact words I'd always wanted to hear: "I love you. I want to marry you someday."

I was sure that the relationship was saving me, when I was the one doing the saving. On some level, I enjoyed cleaning up after him. I guess doing so made me feel important. I faithfully visited and called him when he served time in jail. I rubbed his back when he vomited after drinking too much. I passively shrugged and heaved a deep sigh when Paul would gawk at his calendars and magazines.

Of course, it hurt to be compared to other women, it stung when he yelled, and it upset me when he shoved me just a bit too hard. I was offended when he woke up next to me and didn't remember the night before. I ached when I realized that my life revolved around drinking. "Shouldn't two people who love each other completely, fight rarely?" I asked my diary. Mostly, we argued about his drinking habits. Nevertheless, I still believed I was significant because I was basically someone's liberator.

A friend escorted me to prom senior year because Paul didn't want to go. Being that he was considerably older than I was, he had no interest in a stupid high school dance. I dolled myself up. Paul scolded me and told me I couldn't go because I looked too *good* to be out with another man, even if he was just a friend.

I went. I rebelled. Paul became angry, forceful. But instead of running away, my dreams of leaving him started to fade. I wanted to leave. I knew that I should've been leaving. But for some reason, I couldn't. I didn't.

Every foul inadequacy that I uncovered in a man served to trigger me. My childhood flashbacks haunted me throughout every corrupt relationship that ensnared me. I was entangled in the unrecognized consequences of my complicated past. I not only remembered my past. I also lived in my past. I really couldn't tell which one was which.

Getting caught stealing never made it into my writing. It was documented in the court records, however. A department store worker followed my trail of opened packages. When I was stopped at the door, I pleaded with him to let me pay for the products, but it was too late. As I sat in a room veiled to the public, I felt exposed in my skimpy green tank top. When asked if I'd stolen before, I said I hadn't. But the opposite was true. There'd been so many stealing binges that I couldn't even keep track of the things that I'd taken. What was I hoping to find?

Everyone on my dad's side of the family passively called me a liar by opting to no longer communicate with me the moment he left for prison. Accidentally bumping into any one of my dad's brothers was an awkward, painful, a reminder. I couldn't continue living in that small Wisconsin bubble.

I wanted to leave, start over, forget. College provided me with the opportunity to do so, but Paul followed me there.

On the surface, I confessed my love and need for Paul, but something inside me was perpetually trying to run away. I still longed to receive a promise ring, to be someone's everything. I loathed the way Paul treated me, but I loved the idea of him needing me. If I wanted out so bad, why didn't I just leave?

I knew that life could be better than all that I'd seen, so I applied for scholarships. I finagled my finances so that I could participate in a short-term study abroad program. In the past I hadn't opted to accomplish anything that Paul disapproved of, but this was different. I'd become confident that change was needed, I had a longing to travel, and I was sick of only talking about being free. I was ready to stop talking and start doing, so I left the country for the first time. Without Paul.

I had a remarkable three weeks in Italy and France. I made a new friend. I sun bathed. I photographed my toes in the sand. I ate the most amazing food, gnocchi being my favorite, and tasted real wine—not that cheap, boxed stuff—for the first time. I refrained from shaving my legs. I ate as if my weight was unaffected. My mind was absent of body image frets. I wore the loveliest, Latin-looking, red and orange dress. It was bold, and so was I. I visited the ruins. I gazed in awe of the Catholic cathedrals. It was almost as if I could feel God's presence in the architecture and see God's character in the artwork.

I parasailed over the sea. There weren't many instructions given. Two young men strapped my new friend and I up, clipped us in, and told us to start walking until the wind picked us up. The boat would slow down and dip us in the water. From that high up I could see people in the shadows of the large buildings, going about their business. Parasailing opened the door to feeling like I could do anything. I was distraught to return to Minneapolis, to Paul. I knew what kind of life I was going home to, but at least I'd seen firsthand that freedom could exist.

I was terrified to leave Paul, so I tried to get out by signing an apartment lease without him knowing. I was running the opposite direction in the only way I thought to be safe. I was desperate to convince myself that I'd get along just fine without Paul. If only I could convince myself, but I couldn't without the help of other men.

I'd sneak out of the apartment to spend the night with someone else. I followed another from party to party. I searched for a guy to fill in the gap that'd be present once I said bye to Paul. One of them, Gap Guy, was an acquaintance from high school. He was charming, captivating. We'd stay up for hours fantasizing about traveling to Australia. I leapt from man to man in my vain attempts to achieve the affection I craved so deeply. I guess I just couldn't shake the words of the Goo Goo Dolls, "You bleed just to know you're alive."

Paul certainly didn't believe me when I first told him I was leaving him, and he definitely didn't respond well when he finally grasped that I wasn't going to change my mind. He became angry and hysterical and ultimately stormed out of the apartment. Had me convinced that he was about to do something reckless. I feared for his life and my safety, but I knew I'd made the right choice. I only wish I didn't have to watch him go.

With a crisp, clear mind I applied for nearly 20 scholarships and arranged for some of my courses to be completed in Australia. Admittedly, my actions were somewhat stimulated by my imaginary relationship with Gap Guy, but I still felt liberated when I booked my flights to Australia. I'd leave that upcoming July.

Like most college students, I was working on beefing up my résumé via any means possible at the time. I'd discovered an engineering society and decided to show up to one of the meetings. I arrived promptly on the third floor of one of the older buildings on campus. There, I was greeted by James, a polished man in a suit. His dark eyes and thick hair sent my heart soaring. It was a really bad day to be caught in yoga pants, a messy bun, and post-workout sweat.

There was an entire cheese pizza leftover after the meeting, and James gave that pizza to me. I carried that box over a mile back to my apartment like it was some sort of trophy.

James and I started spending time together. I told him about my dad, something I hadn't done with any of the other guys. And he shared of his own battles. We both knew we were different, nothing like the world around us. I guess we were dating, but we never really labeled ourselves as a couple.

Our relationship quickly became something I wasn't proud of. I knew that something wasn't right. The signs were many: His car was towed when he spent the night at my place. Our time together was sprinkled with speeding tickets and other inconvenient mishaps. Our time apart was bursting with additional aggravations, like me getting stung by a sting ray.

It was as if God was shouting, "Don't do this your way. I know what is best for you! Not now, Kara. Listen to me. Wait."

As I prepared to leave for Australia, I said bye to James. Somehow, I knew I was about to leave my former life behind. If God could take me out of my world to teach me something important once, like He did in Italy and France, why wouldn't He do it again? Mark 1:40 speaks of a man who believed in God's ability to cleanse him. "If you are willing, you can heal me and make me clean" (NLT). Deep down, I think I knew that God was willing. But was I willing to let Him?

Burdened

NO ONE CAN TAKE BACK the things that have happened. It's the worst kind of robbery, the kind where what was stolen can't be returned, the kind of dream where you don't wake up. I was lying there trying to decide if what I saw was real. The most real, vivid, and heart-wrenching dreams were consuming my sleep.

Dad was out of prison, and he was obviously intoxicated. He was only slightly different from the way that I remembered him. He pushed me, negotiated with me, tried to get me into bed with him. I fought, argued, pleaded, and eventually persuaded him to change his mind. Dim lights, dark colors, and blurred shadows surrounded me. I didn't know where I was.

In the dream, my dad never actually touched me, but my fear was severe enough to make it feel like he did. He used his words to brainwash me into thinking that this desired act of his was okay. Evil disguised itself as love and security. I bowed my head in despair. Why me? I clasped my hands together, rested my jaw on them, and allowed my chin to crinkle. My breathing slowed, and I closed my eyes to the chaos.

When I opened them again, I was standing on a deck. My head slowly lifted while my arms lowered down to my side. My shoulders dropped down from my ears. My hair is dark, but the sun summoned bits of red to show. Dandelion seeds rode the waves of the breeze, so I lifted my hands in attempt to catch the falling, fragmented flowers. I was in an elegant snowfall, unaccompanied by the cold. The grass was long and green and stretched far ahead of me, as far as I could see. My dad's brother walked towards me. My uncle is indistinguishable from my father—his face, his gestures—yet he's vastly different. My uncle's smile was inviting, and his hands were open. I ran to him. I tightly wrapped my arms around him as if I'd just found my father.

I whispered into his ear, "I love you." I was overwhelmed by the same safe feeling that I felt when that police officer led me away from my dad.

I longed to run towards my dad, yet I needed to run from him.

A blink was all it took for the sky to darken and for me to go back inside. Dad sat at the far end of the table while I sat opposite of him. A light bulb hung above the table and swung ever so slightly like the pendulum of a clock. It was just enough light to make the center of the table glow, but we both sat in darkness. An eerie hum drowned out my thoughts. Pancakes and syrup begged for my attention and attempted to distract me from the gloom around me, but I didn't dare fall for the diversion. I never touched my tempting breakfast. I only folded my hands, placed them in my lap, and observed my father.

Dad finally lifted his head to steal a glance at me. I quickly responded by making a goofy face at him. It was the same awkward, silly connection that we'd always had, the same connection we faked to ignore what we both knew, deep down, happened.

There I was, sitting next to someone at that table, but that someone didn't have a face. He was only a shadow. But I felt much safer and more comfortable sitting with No Face than I did sitting next to my own father.

Dad continued to read the newspaper and drink his coffee, which aggravated me. I got up, pushed in my chair, walked towards him, and sat down next to him.

In a desperate attempt to fix everything, I pleaded with him. I knew what had to happen in order for us to overcome. I leaned forward and rested my chin on his shoulder. I was careful not to let my body get too close to him. I cupped my hand around his: "Tell me to my face what you did to me."

"Okay," he agreed.

"Please, tell me while you're still sober?" I asked.

"Well that won't last forever," Dad responded.

The honesty was appreciated, the truth sickening. There was never any eye contact. Never. And Dad never told me. No. He never admitted to anything.

Time flickered. I was standing on the deck again. My mom elegantly walked up to me. It was my mother from years ago, young and untouched by my father. It was as if my dad was once the embodiment of all her problems. Then he became the incarnation of mine. Mom appeared to be free from his grasp. She walked off into the woods, alone. Apart from him, she could've been free — she would've been free — but then she wouldn't have had me.

Dad was two people. He was sober, quiet, reserved, consumed with coffee, cooking, and cars. But then he was drunk, persuasive, fascinated by physical highs. Dad was two people, but no matter which person he was, he didn't care much for me.

What a wonderful day it was for a nightmare. Father's Day. The irony wasn't lost on me. It was his day alright, just not in the way I'd longed for it to be.

I can't think of a word for a nightmare that occurs during

the day. A daydream? Never. Torture? The cloud of that dream hovered over the rest of my day—no, my dad's day. It's ironic that your goals and your ambitions, the things that you deeply desire, are called dreams. The visions and flashbacks that haunt your sleep, keep you up late at night, and invade your thoughts are also called dreams. At least not all dreams have to come true.

I was holding Dad's head in the sink. I nearly strangled him, but then I lost my grip and turned to run.

I looked over my shoulder to see him sharpening a large knife. Then running after us. Mom fell, but she got back up. I'll never forget hating him like that. I'd never really hated him, and I never thought I could. But he was chasing me, trying to kill me. Hating him was my only choice.

I was more discombobulated and confused than ever. Was it morning? Night? How long had I been sleeping? I was asleep, wasn't I?

Dad was sitting in his old chair in the old house in that same spot against the far wall. He was using the same lamp and the same reading glasses that I knew so well. His jeans were dark, his legs crossed, his hair unchanged, his eyes aged with bags just as before. He was more real in my dream than he was in real life.

What was the word? What was the word?

Dad sketched the lyrics swiftly and effortlessly as if he was completing a trivial crossword puzzle. He pressed his glasses against his lower lip as if admiring his artwork. The word was "shame." He'd go to Jesus and hand over his shame. He told me he would.

It felt as though I'd worn the clothes before. The yellow shirt and gray capris reminded me of a time when my dad hurt me, but I thought my clothes were new.

Like a shaken-up soda bottle, when I began to speak up, my emotions obnoxiously bubbled over. "We have to get out! We must leave him!" I shouted. I knew that we had to save ourselves, but oh how I wished we could save him too. My anxiety paralyzed me. Was it a warning?

I sat on the edge of my seat. You would've thought it was the football game in front of me that was keeping me on my toes, but it was my dad who was sitting just a couple of rows below. I watched him as he enjoyed the game and failed to notice me. Then he turned, walked toward me. He had something to say.

Someone covered my mouth. "Tell my daughter that I love her," he said to someone that wasn't me. Then a kiss on my forehead.

Dad was so caring. He really cared. But then I opened my eyes.

At a party, Daddy's daughter began to boast about her scandalous clothing. She wasn't me. She was younger, more beautiful. My dad became furious. He ran to her and probed her with questions. He was rather concerned. How had she learned of such indecent attire? Where had she acquired the knowledge to flaunt?

His daughter accused, "Kara—it's Kara's fault! She told me I could."

"That's a lie. I hate who I was then," I negated. "I'm not her anymore!"

With disappointment smeared across his face, my dad scolded, "How could you, Kara? How could you do this? It's all your fault."

All. My. Fault.

My old room at the old house in my hometown. A place for everything, and everything's in its place. All the colors agreed with the ones in my memories. The blue paint on the walls. Dad opened my bedroom door and walked towards me as I lay on my back. I dreaded what he was about to do, but I was helpless.

"Daddy, why are you touching me?" I strained my brain to understand.

"Because I thought you were dead," Dad retorted.

I may as well have been. We argued without rest. I was distraught because I knew that Daddy loved that younger little girl more than me. He'd reached out to protect her, but he was hurting me. He never really loved me.

When he finally left my room, I began to sing. I was surrounded by my blue, sponge-painted walls and bright Christmas lights that hung around the closet frames. "Oh Daddy, please, I can't be your despised, little girl anymore. Oh my father, please, I refuse to be your daughter locked behind closed doors." The song was exquisitely beautiful, every high, low, and pause of the melody still rings in my ears.

I sat in my bed, alone, awake, tormented by my mind.

Confronted

WITH EAGERNESS, I LEFT THE nightmares and the college life behind. Australia was exactly how I'd pictured her to be. With a beer in my hand and a hammock beneath me, I listened to The Cat Empire play by a pool. The palm trees stretched high. The sun shone ever so brightly. And the surf was like a sweet love song sung from a rooftop. The swoosh and crash of each wave serenaded my soul. It all mingled together to create the perfect, carefree day.

I clung to the rush of sky diving and the ease of my new Australian life. There I was, hanging outside of the plane with my legs wrapped under it as if I could've somehow convinced it to save me. At the point of no return, I fell and tumbled, a single seed carried by the wind, so scared, so incredibly happy. I had so far to fall that it didn't even feel like I was falling at all. Time appeared to stand still, and gravity seemed to loosen its grip, at least until I was just about hit the ground.

In Cairns, I was certain I was already experiencing the height of it all. What more could I have asked for? I ventured far away from the boat for well over an hour. There I swam alone among the sea turtles and sea creatures of every kind. The corals tickled my toes, and the sun warmed the clear, blue water just right. But I was wrong, so wrong. Cairns was only the beginning.

I hopped up on my board a few times in the sand before

trying it in the water. I passively floated, gave the waves permission to crash over me as I mentally prepared. I gradually made my way to where the waves began to break. I whipped around and paddled, paddled, paddled before I was lifted up by the surge of a wave. I cautiously stood up. My arms were stiff and straight and my knees were shaky, but I didn't fall.

I quickly adopted the cliché Australian catchphrase "no worries" as my own. There simply wasn't room anymore to dwell on the past, with the beauty of the world at my fingertips. I was seduced, convinced that maybe sadness itself had ceased to exist. I know. Pain is everywhere, but in Australia, I finally wasn't limited by it.

Every day I fought the temptation to be bogged down by the other students. They seemed solely concerned with yet another place to party, yet another place to forget. But for once I wanted to remember. There had to be more to life, and I'd come to a point where I didn't want all the vanity to consume me in the way I saw it consume others. These new understandings made my friends, the people I'd loved and adored, seem like strangers to me.

An Aussie man and I enjoyed a cup of coffee together after I settled into my room. I wasn't sure if it was a date, but I thought it was since he lingered when he said goodbye, and it took him four seconds to ask if he could see me again. His name was Timothy, but I decided to call him Tim. His mom was probably the only person to seriously call him Timothy, along with girls who were trying much too hard to be cute.

Honestly, I didn't want to go. I went to the small gathering hosted by the university's Christian group because Tim was going. The girls that were quick to say hello eased my apprehension. One of them didn't wear any makeup, but her energy and spirit made her attractive. And she never asked me what

I'd done or where I'd been. She only asked me one question with a smile that displayed every tooth: "Do you believe in Jesus?" It was the only thing required of me in order to attend one of their Bible studies. I didn't know it at the time, but in that moment, I said yes to the most important question I'd ever be asked.

I told this girl that I did, in a soft, unsure sort of way. I did believe, but I hadn't voiced that conviction in years. And I certainly never acted much like I believed. There came a time when I was much too dirty for church. They didn't want me. I didn't want them. The abuse wasn't spoken of, and my mother's divorce wasn't supported in my childhood church. I'd assumed all those years that God was just as disapproving.

A pastor of mine once likened the mercy of the cross to a flood. Imagine that the God of the universe has decided to flood the entire world as He did in the time of Noah. He's decided to wipe out every human being because He can no longer bear the sin. (God's made a covenant with us that there won't be another flood, but for the sake of the analogy let's pretend that a flood is coming.)

And the rain begins to pour. After a few days, the water begins to creep up to your ankles. And after a week, you're submerged up to your waist. Walking anywhere is a drag. Your most prized possessions are being marinated in dirty, grimy, sewer water. Soon, your toes can no longer touch the bottom, which quickly shifts all concern from your belongings to your survival. The water climbs to the tops of the buildings, even the tallest ones. The moments between treading water and becoming overly exhausted seem to linger on forever. With every hour, every shower increases the distance between you and the earth.

Large beasts have traveled from oceans afar and they now

lurk beneath you. Then night falls. The stars provide very little light on this new moon night. Then it happens. You see a lifeless body float past you. Many more follow — adults, children, animals. They're all gone except for a straggling few. You begin to wonder. What will kill you? A creature? The fear? The anxiety? The frigid water? Dehydration? Starvation? Then even the air stops moving. A storm must be coming, perhaps an enormous hurricane.

Suddenly, you see a light in the distance. From where you are, it looks like a firefly, but slowly, ever so slowly, it grows. So does your hope. In fact, the light moves towards you. Is that a boat!?

You wail in your helplessness, "Over here! Over here!" And just as a shark swims past, a ladder plummets into the water only a few feet away. You bolt. At the top of the ladder, a strong hand reaches and pulls you up, wraps you in a blanket, feeds you, and fills your soul in every way. The hours to follow are filled with joy, gladness, and disbelief as you celebrate with other survivors.

Then your rescuer speaks to you: "Dear child, you are precious to me. You are beautiful. There's no one else like you. You fill me with joy." You rest in the comfort of someone who feels like an old family friend, though you've never met him before. Your gladness peaks when the clouds clear, revealing a sunrise in the distance.

"My dear child, I wish I could stay with you, but I can't. For you to stay, I must go. Remember me, and follow my ways always. I love you." Just as he speaks his last words to you, he steps onto the railing and slowly falls backwards. He willingly dies a terrible death, alone in the open water. And you're left to wonder, *Why me? I did nothing to deserve this.* You didn't. In fact, you are the reason he had to jump. Sin pushed him. Sin killed him. My sinner soul deserved to drown in a flood, but that isn't what happened. He saved me. I only needed to let Him save me. You've read what I turned to, and yet there's a way out. Grace. When that girl asked me if believed in Jesus, I said yes to grace.

"Great! I'm so excited! We meet Tuesdays at seven. Bring your Bible."

Except when I packed for Australia, "bring my Bible" wasn't on the top of my priority list next to "get drunk" and "find a boyfriend as soon as possible." I did have one at home, but I'd kept it mostly because it had my name imprinted on it, and it'd been pushed to the back of the bookshelf. I made quite a big deal out of finding a Bible for my new study group. It took nearly two hours to choose which version to buy, and I wouldn't leave the store without finding a suitable case for it.

I met missionaries from Minnesota and Wisconsin. I fell in love with Jesus when I saw how accepted I was among them, but under the full weight of confrontation, I suddenly felt a lot of anger towards men. It appeared that they all had one warped goal with me all along, and I *welcomed* them. In acknowledging this, I began to carry the heavy burden of my many mistakes. I despised the deception I'd seen. I detested my sin, and yet somehow, I still felt joy. Despite all the horrendous memories. It was the joy that reassured me. I knew it had to be God.

I began to grab a hold of my purpose in life, even if I didn't fully comprehend what that purpose was. I saw that my prayers had power and my presence was intentional. I clung to this: The purpose is always greater than the pain that paves the way.

I started praying for my family. I asked that God would do for them what He was doing for me. Instead of wondering why the abuse had to happen to me, I wondered why I was the one who got to live a life of traveling and adventure. I felt sort of undeserving of what I was being given. I wanted my family to experience those gifts too, so I entered my mom into a contest to win a trip to New Zealand.

The challenge was to explain with a video why my single parent deserved the trip. I created a slide show of sentimental pictures and the words of my heart. My mom was my backbone, the only one who urged me to stand up for myself.

When I learned that the entry was chosen as a finalist, I jumped vigorously up and down on my bed before bolting down the street to the nearest pay phone so I could share the news with my mom. My energy radiated into the air around me, and my excitement was sensed by the people walking past me. When my mom didn't win the trip, the letdown was just as dramatic. But maybe that video was more than a contest entry. Maybe it served to remind me of what I could be thankful for: my mom.

I'd never felt so sheltered and protected from harm. The chances of my father finding me, hurting me, or deceiving me there were about the same as finding pure gold on the sidewalk. It wasn't going to happen. My dad's parole stipulations didn't allow him to leave the country, let alone my hometown.

My black-and-white view of men was slowly starting to fade. One of the missionaries walked me home at night to protect me, not to pursue me. A gentle Chinese man enjoyed jalapeño pepper eating contests with me to laugh with me, not to flirt with me. Every man I met through this Christian group warmly encouraged my participation in their ultimate Frisbee games. These men guarded me. I wasn't sure why, but they didn't exploit me.

There was a stretch on the campus trail that caused my

feet to linger and my camera to stutter whenever I went running. And when I ran, time didn't exist. That path was where I first became fond of being alone. It was a new kind of alone. It was voluntary and peaceful, and I was unafraid. I was often submerged in sun drenched, glowing greens and greeted by curious lizards, vibrant parrots, and hand-sized spiders.

I never wanted to forget my new sanctuary, so I hung my camera on a nearby branch, set the timer, and darted as the beep began to sound. I captured the ridiculous sight of me popping out from behind a bush as if I'd been hiding, but I was pleased that the image adequately depicted my joy.

I brought my Bible with me to that study and pretended that I had it all along. No one noticed, and they were just as clueless about my past. I had a secret, and for the first time it was mine to tell, so I did. I was entirely comfortable in my own skin as if I'd never experienced the darkness of shame. A new comfort accompanied me, one that included sweat pants and excluded makeup. There was no one to impress, no one to disappoint.

But you know that song, *Dark Side of the Moon*? Unfortunately, my heart had a dark side too. Tim and I argued so much I was half-convinced that Paul had followed me to Australia. Tim was a baby Christian, and I can't say I blame him. I was a new Christian too, and neither of us knew what we were doing. Tim understood that part of being an unmarried Christian was not having sex, but he didn't understand why. He was employing the Try Very Hard Not to Do It approach. So between his desire for sex and my warped need for intimacy, we bent the rules but didn't break them, which left me more puzzled than ever. He told me that he *could* love me one day, but I knew that he didn't, that he wouldn't. And even though the decision was half-mine, I still felt valued for only my body again. I didn't want to lose myself. I didn't want to go back to where I'd been.

I was radically caught up in the drama of my new Christian dating experience, but the aftermath of my childhood wasn't lost on me. I prayed that God would forgive my dad, that He'd be with him through his transition out of prison and back into life in the real world. I still loved my dad, and that's how I started to understand how God could love me, even after all the horrendous things I'd done.

I managed to escape for a few days to the Blue Mountains on a volunteer excursion. I missed Tim, but the distance was a breath of fresh air. In the absence of mirrors, spending the weekend with gym clothes and without beauty products didn't bother me. A bug even bit me beneath my eye while I slept. My eye swelled severely. I resembled a drunken pirate the next day, but no one looked at me any different. In the evenings, I played my guitar. It was the first time I'd let anyone hear my playing, and I returned from that volunteer trip having gained even more than I'd given: a little love for myself.

The next morning, the powerful sun commanded me to get out of bed. It teamed up with the obnoxious, squawking bird right outside my window to be sure that I didn't fall back asleep. Then a voice spoke to me, not audible but clear. I can't explain how I knew, but I was certain that my relationship with Tim was about to end, like its purpose had already been fulfilled. Ten minutes later, I was dumped and hunched over on the sidewalk. Another five and I was crying hysterically on my lump of a dorm bed. But I prayed, clutched my Bible as if it were a teddy bear, and fell asleep. And when I went to church again, I knew for sure it wasn't because of Tim. I began to act out of my own faith instead of borrowing from his.

It was Father's Day in Australia. When I approached the church entrance, I spotted a line of remodeled cars, and I was jolted back to when my dad and I used to wander between the rows of cars at old car shows. During the service, I felt as if the pastor was speaking directly to me. He acknowledged that for some, Father's Day serves only to commemorate a significant loss, sometimes a harsh one. I drank from the communion cup that day for the first time in eight years. This conventional expression of faith was the most soothing of ceremonies for me. It was one that acknowledged the letting go of all that Father's Day used to signify for me and all that it'd never mean to me. And in that moment, I understood that God was asking me to write a letter to my dad to declare my love and forgiveness.

So there I was, full of freedom, faith, and all kinds of zeal. And then I caught wind via the up-and-coming social media venue, Facebook, that Gap Guy had just landed in Australia and was staying at a nearby university. Since he's part of this story, I'm going to give him a real name, though I can't say I want to. How about Jordan? His presence in Australia confused me. I arrived first. I was accepted into the study abroad program long before he planned his trip. I didn't go to Australia for Jordan. I was, like, 60 percent sure of this. There other 40 percent considered it destiny.

I was ready to leave the city for a few days and join a few friends on an adventure to Fraser Island. The hostel near the departure point was unexpectedly closed for the evening, so we gathered our sleeping bags and headlamps and parked our bodies on the beach for the night. Illegal? Apparently. But I was more concerned with animals pilfering our food or playing with our hair in the middle of the night.

In the morning, we hopped on a boat and then piled into a

couple of jeeps. The water was far clearer than my mind. Boxed wine disguised my faith in Jesus. No one would've ever guessed that He was my God. By nightfall, I was *her* again, my old self at a tantalizing party. The sun went down along with my convictions. Dingo dogs began to roam the shoreline.

A week prior, I captivated the crowd with my music, but all Jordan needed was two minutes and a harmonica to whip everyone's attention back around to himself. I wasn't so surprised. He was rather charming, just like my dad. As I laid my head down on Jordan's lap, I recited his lyrics along with him. Our voices harmonized. I wished our hearts would do the same.

Jordan and I shared a tent for the night. I wanted to use his arm as a pillow, but he appeared to be uninterested in my snuggling. So I rolled over, turned my back to him, crossed my arms, and passively agreed to play the game. I waited until the snores came before resting my head on his arm.

The beauty of the Lord's creations mixed with the gravity of my sin made for a neutral weekend. I acknowledged God's wonder. I gazed in awe of the massive cliffs and the landscapes, yet I became jealous of the girls around me who were thinner and, in my opinion, therefore prettier. I danced in the morning. I celebrated the sunrise and my shadow on the beach before anyone was up, and yet I ached for approval. The blend made my emotions turn pale.

Days later, I felt so much like a child and so much like an adult at the same time. I could remember who I was before. I remembered what it was like to have respect for myself. I'd almost forgotten what it was like to be with a man, and I liked not remembering.

Celebrating my birthday with the missionary girls was reminiscent of a childhood sleepover. They baked me a cake, candles and all, and sang to me. I know I'm not supposed to tell, but when I blew out the candles on that birthday cake, I wished to always trust God. I could feel their love for me just by being in the same room with them. Where was all the love coming from? When prayed for at dinner, I saw myself as a harmless little girl, maybe for the first time ever. I was 21, and yet I blew out my candles as if I was 12 again. All negativity, the memories of my many mistakes, all worries. Gone. I felt at home, with family. I was even comfortable enough to fall asleep on a couch foreign to me. Maybe my life is just backwards, 21 at 12 and 12 at 21. I was an adult my whole childhood, and then just as I was coming of age, I finally got to become the kid I never got to be.

The next day, I headed to the beach. I was surrounded by people but felt all alone. Just me, my music, the sun, and the sound of the waves. I paused for a moment, curled my toes in the sand, and froze a frame of them, just like I'd done in France. Most 21st birthday extravaganzas in America are about embracing the freedom to drink, but I considered myself above the let's-all-get-stupid-drunk tradition. Instead, I surfed until Jordan met up with me on the beach. I reassured myself that spending time with him was fine. I wasn't explicitly doing anything wrong, but what I didn't realize was I was opening a door to something I wouldn't have the strength to close later that night.

We went to a romantic Italian café where we ate gnocchi and drank wine. I shared stories about my time in Italy. Afterwards, Jordan bought me whiskey as a birthday present. Whiskey was always an attention-grabber, a command that I be noticed, a plea that I be admired. Then I played my guitar for him. I sang *Redemption Song*. He played *The Wind* by Cat Stevens. We conversed for hours about a myriad of topics. We even talked about sex, when it should be present in a relationship and when it shouldn't. And there it was: my chance. A door had opened for me to tell him about my faith and all about how I'd changed.

I told him my new stance about sex and sort of included God, but I didn't exactly declare my beliefs. I said something like, "Being sexual confuses the motives of a relationship and if that line is crossed, I can't tell anymore. I've just decided not to have sex anymore." I was furious with myself! Was I denying God? Why was I so afraid to declare my love for God? Why was I so concerned with Jordan's disapproval of me?

"Oh…sure. Yeah, I hate conveying the wrong message," Jordan agreed. At least that's the way I saw it at the time.

Feeling safe in our conversation, I continued to drink. Then he kissed me. He said he wrote a song for me and when he sang it, I melted into a puddle on the floor as if he was the sun and I was snow, and I was only doing that which came most naturally. Was it love? Regrettably, I altogether stopped consuming the whiskey, and it started to consume me. He was the sun, and I was revolving. One swift line was all it took for me to become paralyzed in his bed.

I understood what being happy meant. The magazines, the movies. I understood that touch and flattering remarks from a man were stamps of approval, ones that defined my worth. I'd been taken, tossed, used, and thrown away just like any other disposable pleasure product that virtually all convenience stores offer. Through sexual abuse, it was communicated to me that my worth simply wasn't beyond my body. Trapped in a dream, a nightmare, everything I thought would never happen to me, happened. Even the things I couldn't have imagined happened. I ran. I cried out. I screamed at the top of my lungs, but no one seemed to hear me. I wasn't even sure I could hear myself. I could feel the cry in my throat, but when I opened my mouth, silence. Nothing.

I wanted to fight. Really, I did. But I woke up under the weight of heavy sheets. I swore off ever touching a man again. I was looking for a birthday that would mark a big decision, a leap of change. That day guided me towards a revolution, just not in the most ideal of ways.

It amazes me how God forgives you even when you can't forgive yourself. Our sin costs more than we could ever pay. It devastates more than we could ever imagine and progresses far beyond what we ever intend. I knew I crossed God's line that night, and I couldn't wrap my mind around the fact that God didn't hate me for it. A confession didn't feel like enough, like it barely scratched the surface. But John 1:9 says, "But if we confess our sins, he will forgive our sins, because we can trust God to do what is right. He will cleanse us from all the wrongs we have done." To plead guilty after being forgiven is to deny the power of God.

That sinking feeling in my chest prompted me to ask God for clarity regarding my relationships. I asked to know the truth, and when I found Jordan, I boldly confronted him about the nauseating nature of our birthday encounter. My voice softened, but my posture maintained adequate brashness. "Jordan, I think that what we did last night was wrong."

"Well, it's simple. We're never going to be together if that's how you think," Jordan responded, his voice void of all emotion, his words the exact opposite of everything I'd longed to hear. How'd I get dumped when I didn't even *have* a boyfriend in the first place? It was then that I began to see it: Even when I complied, I walked away empty handed. Every time.

One small decision—a prayer, a thought, a glance—can change everything. A single conversation with Gap Guy over a drink one night planted the seed of Australia. On my birthday, I saw an art sale and decided to invest in some old canvases and paints. And I'd brought a guitar with me to Australia, which led me learning heaps of songs. These were the little things that God placed in my life to help carry me through this confusing and challenging time. The strings of my guitar started to glisten. I deleted phone numbers along with a lot of temptation in my life. I'd never felt so strong, and not by my power, but by the hand of God. I stayed up all night soaking it in and pouring it out.

Daddy

I was five years
When you first heard me cry
I never wanted to say goodbye
But you let me go, you knew it was true
Whatever is real will always come back, to you
Sometimes I can't believe you're here with me
My life's fitting together so perfectly
And it's only through your love
That I can really see
All I'll ever need is you loving me, Daddy
I was in high school when I first denied
And more days than not I just sat down and cried
But you held on tight and forgave me always
That kind of love is tough to find, I'd say
I got caught up in the pain and kept it all inside
I cheated, I stole, and often-times I lied
I even tried to love many men
More than I love you
I didn't think your heart would end up
Breaking, in two

*Now I've really grown up
And my dreams are staying strong
I'm glad to be back, Dad it's been too long
If I didn't have you in my life
I don't know what I would do
All I'm trying to say Daddy is
Thank you, I love you*

The soggy sand squished between my toes. My seashell collection was becoming too large to fit into the palm of my hand. As I picked up each shell, I noticed each detail: the crevasses, the colors, the cracks. I admired my seashells despite their imperfections, maybe even because of them. I brought my handful of shells to the ocean and let the water pour over them, cleansing them of the dirt. I saw to it that none of them drifted out to sea. They were mine. And I knew I was God's. He was constantly picking me up, dusting me off, and working on my imperfections.

During my final church service in Australia, the pastor cried as he spoke on the topic of sexual abuse. It was almost as if I could visualize Jesus doing the same thing. I'd found freedom, closure, and closeness, and I didn't want to leave. Would I be able to bottle up all that had taken place in Australia and take it home with me? I was afraid to go home. Afraid I wouldn't have the strength. Afraid because my dad had been released from prison. But the beautiful magnificence of New Zealand at my fingertips was enough to make me forget about my reality. At least for a little while.

Unbound

MY REMINISCENT LAUGHS SOON TURNED into regretful sobs as I said goodbye to the friends I'd made and the places I'd come to love. I said farewell to the beach, my room, the trail, and the campus as if they were people too. My guitar and I were the only ones to ever claim that room, and that bed for that matter. I was proud of that.

Since there was a week between my final exams and my departing flight, I stayed with a friend's parents, the Wilsons. They cooked dinner for me every night. I was allowed a glass of wine with dinner, which made me feel like I'd been promoted to a whole new level of adult. Mr. Wilson played pool with me. He even took me to hear a band play at a local pub. When I was out with Mr. Wilson, I let everyone assume that I was his daughter. I even played my guitar for them.

I had the strongest sense that an unimaginable adventure was about to take place, one that I couldn't fathom. I sat at a bench before checking in at the airport. I was so very alone, so bizarrely relaxed. And for a moment, I waited as if I had someone to say goodbye to. The image of leaving for Australia only five months prior was suspended before me: I kept looking back until I could no longer see my mom. Oddly enough, I was wearing the same baby blue t-shirt that I'd worn the day I left, only I didn't have anyone to wave to.

I gathered my things and began making my way to my gate. I was surrounded by so many people, but they weren't as scary as they'd once been. The composed peace let me know that I was finally on track with God's plan and not my own. I was purely and simply following Him. To New Zealand of all places.

After boarding, a young man in a large straw hat and a blue button-up shirt sat down next to me. His shirt was classy, but he dressed it down by leaving it un-tucked and pairing it with jeans. I chose not to make it obvious that I'd noticed him. I continued to hunch over my journal that rested on the flip-down table in front of me until he said something. We knew each other in a way only two travelers could. He was poised and worldly, soon to be a permanent resident of New Zealand. Then we sat in silence as we soared among the clouds.

"How did someone like yourself afford to come here?" A Customs security officer probed.

"I paid for it myself," I answered.

"Why are you here? What are you doing here?" the officer asked, determined to stump me.

"It's New Zealand. Who wouldn't want to come here? I'll be traveling around for a few weeks."

"North or South Island?" he asked.

"Both."

"Who do you know here?"

"I don't know anyone."

"Who booked the car?"

"I did," I responded with confidence.

"Who planned this trip?"

"I did." I did? The corners of my mouth slowly turned upwards until a wide grin covered my entire face. "Sir, I did! I planned this trip."

Stamp!

"Enjoy your trip, Miss Mendez."

Auckland to Lake Taupo

My flight landed around midnight, so I had eight hours to kill. I pushed three chairs together and created a bed for myself on the upper level of the airport. My sweatshirt was on backwards over my arms for a blanket. The glass windows were smeared with rain, my guitar case propped up against them. I tucked my arm underneath my head and gazed out the window at the red, blurry plane lights.

After hours of fading in and out, I stepped outside for the first time. The sky was grey and dark, but somehow everything still glowed. The greens were more vivid than anything I'd ever seen. The air was crisp and cool and pure. Untouched. After two hours of waiting, a large van picked me up.

"I've never driven on the left side of the road," I confessed. "I guess I shouldn't have told you that?"

"Ah, you'll be fine, eh. We get people like you in here all the time. You'll get used to it." How reassuring!

I signed a piece of paper. He handed me the keys, and I was challenged to make a graceful departure from the parking lot. After placing my bags in the trunk of the hatchback, I started the car, took a few deep breaths, and pulled out onto the road without looking back. The first stoplight tested my brain's ability to do a complete 180. *Okay, stay to the left...turn right...but don't turn into the right lane!* My panic started to dissipate once I made it to the freeway.

I ventured further away from Auckland, away from the buildings, away from civilization. Each kilometer traveled brought me closer to greener terrain and more mountainous landscapes. After the sweat finally dried from the steering wheel, I stopped at a grocery store to stock up. I filled my cart with the basic survival items: wool socks, trash bags, cereal, a loaf of bread, carrots, kiwi fruit, chips, jam, peanut butter, five noodle packages, four granola bars, three rolls of toilet paper, two cans of pineapple slices, one donut, one can of tomato soup, one energy drink, one lighter, and one plastic bowl. I placed everything in the passenger seat. Behold, my kitchen for an entire month.

After just a few short hours, Motorway 1 elevated me to another world. Every page in my *Lonely Planet* book was covered with highlights, noted possible destinations, but my research didn't make deciding where to stop any simpler. In fact, it complicated matters. My research simply made me aware of the many places I'd have to say no to.

I spotted a sign for Huka Falls and decided to pull over. The falls were heavenly, so white yet so vibrantly blue, so blue yet so luminously green. They gradually and gently blended into a powerful yet peaceful river.

Another ten minutes in the car brought me to Craters of the Moon. That's when I caught glimpses of the first set of snowcapped mountains I'd ever seen. At the same time, steam rolled up from beneath the earth's surface. The fog-like mist hovered just above the ground. Bubbles floated up from the mud. The time was unknown and irrelevant to me. I would soon lose track of the days.

I decided to spend my first night at a hostel in Taupo. The money was well worth it for a bed and a kitchen, especially since I hadn't really slept in 48 hours. I informed the front desk that I'd be leaving well before their office opened. Though exhausted, I walked the single kilometer down to the lake. My lounging and journaling was uninterrupted, and the sunset was invigorating.

I wondered why a place like that wasn't flooded with people. Everything I'd seen appeared to be uncontaminated. I reasoned that New Zealand's a relatively young country due to recent tectonic plate shifts. God's still creating it, and people just haven't had enough time to mess it up yet.

Lake Taupo to Picton

In a haze, I pulled out onto the right side of the road at 4:30 a.m. Luckily, I quickly remembered where I was and swerved over to the left. Imagining the mountains through the clouds and fog just wasn't the same as seeing them, so I drove a lot that first full day. And since any given radio station remained static-free for only two minutes at a time, I put on a sermon. "Remember what God has done for you! Things will get tough. There will be temptations and tests along the way." I'd heard the words before, but they began to take on a new meaning. I was very aware of the struggles that would come.

I made a wrong turn that sent me on quite the detour and ultimately landed me on Foxton Beach. The sky and waves were dark and powerful, yet the absence of the sun oddly didn't subtract from the beauty of the beach. Like a child, I gladly accepted the joy that God had stored up for me. I grabbed my guitar and walked along the water until my car became an ant in the distance. My diet that day consisted of two pieces of jelly toast, kiwi fruit, a bag of chips, a beer, a coffee, and a peanut butter and jelly sandwich—yuck—but the sacrifice was minor compared to all that I was experiencing. I played a few songs and recorded a couple of videos before the rain picked up, a signal for me to resume my travels.

The man behind the Picton ferry counter and I chatted as I booked a ticket for the 3 a.m. ferry. He was from Northern Wisconsin too! What are the odds? I was constantly reminded that I'd soon have to return to reality.

I had six hours to kill before I'd need to drive my hatchback onto the boat, so I chose to walk the streets of Wellington in search of a calling card. I was eager to deliver a trip report to my mom. Her voice brought the security of a best friend, one who always listened. She sounded well. I hoped she really was.

The chilly breeze and misty rain pushed me into a Christian book store, and I immediately spotted a ring in the shape of a cross. A kind woman with greying hair offered to unlock the case for me, so I tried it on. A flawless fit, elegant shine. Finding the ring secured my conviction. Any man wanting to date me would see it and to pursue me, he'd have to agree with its purpose. It was a symbol of my covenant with God. I bought the ring and wore it proudly on the only finger it fit on, my ring finger.

I'd read about a jazz bar on Cuba Street, so I set out to find it. A man played a fiddle in the street. His case wide open next to him requested donations. But to my surprise, the jazz bar turned out to be an old Irish pub.

"Kia ora!" A young guy greeted me at the door.

"Kia what?" I asked with confusion that was far from flattering.

"Hello there!"

I asked the guy if the place had a dress code, and he looked at me like I was crazy. I really don't know what I was thinking. Bars don't have dress codes. But my wool socks were hiked up to my knees. I also had dingy tennis shoes, a drenched hoodie, and dirty leggings.

I ordered a beer and sat down to write in my journal. It wasn't long before I slid my hand under my thigh to cover up the sparkling finger. I was all too aware that such a display could ruin my chances for romance. I mean, my apparent unpredictable lack of ability to maintain self-control was *why* the ring was there. I looked down at the ring and heard what it had to say: "Jesus, I'm yours, and I want the world to see," so that's what I did. I began to beam, wave it around like a fresh fiancé would, and do everything but say, "Look at me, look at me!" as I left the pub.

I knew I would've been back to the old ways in that pub if weren't for God. I knew it was His strength, not mine. And I wasn't afraid. I stopped abruptly and sat on the curb because I realized something right then. God planned that trip for me, and I was simply executing it. Like a small plant undergoing photosynthesis, I soaked up the light of God's grace while I rested on that dirty, dingy sidewalk. My world was made of cement, but I started to see green poke up through the cracks.

I caught a few hours of sleeps in the back seat of the hatchback before boarding the ferry in the middle of the night. You probably think I knew exactly what I was doing, but I didn't. I was a boy scout impersonator. Admittedly, I did feel slightly sheepish with my sleeping bag around me and my red hoodie over me. I was also holding my cute, butterfly notebook. *Somewhere over the Rainbow* was playing on my iPod. You'll see though, I got good at being alone in the wilderness.

The adrenaline kept me from falling asleep. A movie was playing a few rows away from where I was engulfed in my sleeping bag, so I hobbled on over as if I was competing in a potato sack race. Two young men and a young woman were sitting in the front row. They were quick to say hello. The short-haired woman who was probably only a couple of years older than me gave me her number and offered to show me around the North Island. The men acted like her sidekicks.

And then she lent me her jacket when I said I was cold, a drink when I mentioned I was thirsty. I guess it was a mistake to accept the jacket, but I'd assumed that she was just being welcoming and outgoing. Yes, me taking her jacket gave her the green light. I soon started to recognize the sexual overtone in her language, that I was being hit on. By a woman. That was…new. And weird. And honestly, kind of nice.

The rest of the night was a blur. Three hours felt like eight. I faded in and out for the last hour before arriving in Picton at 6 a.m. The green, steep mountains on either side of the canal were alluring, even though they were somewhat distorted by the fog. After several requests, I posed for a picture with my admirer. No doubt, I did enjoy hearing her tell me I was beautiful.

Picton was charming, especially down by the harbor that was bursting with blossoming flowers, palm trees, and an insane number of ducks. The light coverage of my fleece jacket convinced me to wait out the rain at a nearby café and enjoy some breakfast—enough eggs, toast, pancakes, and coffee to satisfy a small army of men. The day had barely arrived, but I could no longer fight the urge to keep moving. I left Picton after buying a poncho and shrugging at the nonexistent sun.

Picton to Fox Glacier
The roads made it downright impossible to tell if I was traveling north, south, east or west. I was constantly turning left, right, up, down, and all over the place. I was totally car sick. Between that and my resolve to not let the rain hinder my trip, I stopped. The Queen Charlotte Trek consisted of a dirt trail surrounded by massive tall trees. The solitude was quite random. The only people I bumped into were the two I saw exiting the trail just as I was entering. We laughed at each other, acknowledging our shared love for crazy.

There were windows between the bushes where I could peek out. (I actually *hate* that word. That's what the judge called it. He "peeked" at me in the shower. It just sounds so degrading, and I'm pretty sure it was more than a peek.) But through these openings, I could see the deep blue water and a long strip of mountains. The self-portraits I took captured droplets of water as they fell. The frozen bits of water around my face resembled diamonds. I was glowing. After a 45-minute hike, I kicked my muddy shoes against the car door and continued driving south.

Ten minutes outside of Nelson I prayed for sunshine, and by the time I arrived, not a single cloud disrupted the sky. I paused there to acquire an autograph from the son of *The Lord of the Rings* ring maker. As I drove farther, the snowcapped mountains appeared to grow. My eyes became fixated on the mountains, nothing else.

In a mesmerized, mirage-chasing daze, I drove completely out of the way and about emptied my gas tank. After sighing at the site of the mountains in my rear-view mirror, I caught a glimpse of a partially hidden gravel road. Without hesitation, I committed to a bit of off-roading. A fire pit rested at the bottom of the steep, dodgy path. Someone must've camped there before. I wasn't sure how safe or legal it was, but I was fairly hidden from the main road.

I assembled my tent and started to gather some fire wood. When I looked up, I saw the first car that I'd seen all day. I rushed into the bushes and ducked, not wanting to be seen. It quickly became a game, one of remaining hidden and facing my fear of being alone in the dark.

I felt obligated to shower at this point, since it'd been four or five days, so I put on my swimsuit. I posed in front of the car window and took a picture of my reflection because I was about to bathe in a nearly frozen river. Submerging myself was paralyzing. The river was without a doubt sub-bearable, so I quickly scrubbed up, bolted back to the car, and changed my clothes. It was enough to carry me through a few more days.

I was constantly on the move. I was hungry and desperate for real sleep, so I heated up a can of tomato soup over my fire that I couldn't have been more proud of. When the darkness began to settle, I moved to my tent. I rested on my stomach, kicked my feet up in the air, and grinned. Noteworthy boy scout skills: I didn't have any legitimate cooking supplies, and yet I was fed by a warm meal. I felt so profoundly cool as I journaled by the light of my orange headlamp.

In the morning, I packed up my things, wet as they were, and said goodbye to my much-loved campsite. The jaunt up the steep hill was daunting. When I started gaining traction, I floored it and didn't look back. My nerve proved effective, and I made it to the gas station about 30 kilometers past empty.

I was sure that the waterfalls rushing down the sides of the mountains were coming straight from heaven. The numerous one-lane bridges along the way caused me to squeal in minor bouts of panic, but at least they led me to the Tauranga Bay Seal Colony. The bluffs guzzled up the coastline. A cruel kiwi bird stole my sandwich, but the seals played and carried on as if they were unaware of my presence.

The penguin crossing signs I saw along the way warned me that I was entering a whole new territory. I paused for a moment to refer to my *Lonely Planet* book. I barely had enough time to read the words "Truman Track" before I recognized them on the sign directly ahead of me. A boot-shaped pillar was positioned in the distance apart from the aid of man. The water had eroded away bits of the coast.

I was more than satisfied with the small town I ended up in for the night. The hostel was neatly tucked atop a jewelry store. I could see the Alps from the window next to my bed, and the beach was just a short walk away. Christmas was just around the corner, but you never would've guessed it apart from the small, fake pine tree that decorated the common area. And sure, I had chills, but it wasn't because I was cold. It was because I was being given so much.

I'd removed my socks only once up until this point, so a real shower was both a necessity and a hard-earned luxury. Afterwards, I cooked up some noodles with the kind of expertise one can only glean from being in college. Then I grabbed a drink and headed down to the beach to watch the sunset. Submerged in warmth, relaxation, comfort, and cleanliness, I stayed until the sun went down. And the clouds didn't hinder the sunset. They actually enhanced it.

The drive continued to leave me dumbfounded. The snow-cloaked mountains were like angels to me. They never lost their invigorating effect.

During my hike to the base of the Franz Josef Glacier, I was convinced I was tramping around in circles. I couldn't seem to get any closer to the immense, semi-stationary iceberg. And with a lush forest behind me, a frozen world ahead of me, a waterfall to my right, and many barren cliffs and boulders to my left, I seemed to be standing in the center of all seasons. After hesitating for over an hour, I decided to proceed and travel the 23 kilometers south to Fox Glacier to set up camp for the night.

My tent neatly neighbored the Southern Alps, and Fox Glacier Guiding was within walking distance. I reserved a space for the ice climbing trip in advance, so I wouldn't be able to change my mind. A nap helped to calm my nerves. The sun soaking through the top of my tent created a relaxing sauna effect. I played my guitar and watched the sunset dance from Mount Tasman to Mount Cook.

The cold woke me up at 4 a.m., so I sprinted to the facility building to have a hot shower. I timed my morning visit to Lake Matheson perfectly. I arrived at the optimal lookout point two minutes before the sun began to creep up over the top of the mountains. Light from the far side of the mountains began to brighten the sky, but when I returned to my campsite, I saw that the town remained in the shadows until much later in the morning.

Myself and seven others congregated in the lobby of the guiding lodge. We were an eccentric collection of travelers. All ages, different home countries, with and without companions. Our thirst for adventure was the only common thread. I stuffed my bag with a set of crampons, two ice axes, ginger cookies, and a sandwich. I decorated myself with two hats, gloves, a jacket, hiking boots, a helmet, and socks that were even more manly than the ones I'd been wearing.

I took a trip to the loo, mostly to ensure that I looked okay with all the gear on. Did I really have to wear a baseball cap? The guides assured me it was necessary because even though it'd be cold, the sun would still insist on cooking my face. But I was sure they were being overdramatic. I also opted not to smear sunscreen on top of my makeup. This was because I'd noticed one of my guides lingering near me when I was getting ready. He was tall, dripping with a fresh New Zealand accent.

When I emerged from the bathroom, I bumped into one of my Fraser Island friends. We posed for a picture, giddy with shock. She was traveling with friends and invited me to come along. I decided to continue on alone. Then I boarded the bus.

It cost me 800 patiently climbed steps to make it to the base of the ice where I started videotaping my every move. I was mid-glacier-pan when I was scolded like a school girl for not paying attention to my guide, so I strapped on my crampons and started practicing on a gentle slope. *Crunch, crunch, crunch.*

After a short tramp upwards, my guide secured the carabiners for my first climb. It amazed me that metal spikes less than one inch long could hold my body weight. The tip of one crampon supported me. My axe penetrated the ice ever so slightly, and I pulled myself up. I had no choice but to trust Mason, the guide who was belaying me. He cheered me on steadily. He showed me where to place my toes and reminded me to keep my arms straight. And when I handed Mason my camera, our hands touched.

With each hack of my ice axe, I gained confidence until I was ultimately lowered into a crevasse of clear blue ice. Water soaked through my jacket, and my muscles twitched under the strain. A river water rushed underneath the ice passionately. I climbed out carefully.

The walk down was a relief compared to the hike up. As I breezed down the steps, Jack, one of the guides, offered me a place to sleep for the night. I gave him a cool, cheeky smile as I slowly removed my hat.

"Does the sight of my terribly sun-burned face change your mind?" I asked.

Jack laughed. "You can barely tell. And no, it doesn't bother me one bit."

Jack was probably in his thirties (which seemed old and border-line creepy to me at the time), with a grungy style and a lonely heart, but I gave him the benefit of the doubt and agreed to swing by his place after gathering my things from the camp site. A couch to sleep on and a hot shower was an offer that I couldn't pass up...And maybe I'd "accidentally" bump into Mason later that evening.

Mason chose not to sit next to me during the ride back into town. While I considered it a bummer, I moved forward with my stalker-I-like-you-please-notice-me plan of action. Jack drew me a map to his house while Mason appeared to be distracted with putting our equipment away. I loitered, hoping that'd he'd say bye, but he didn't. After five minutes, I couldn't sacrifice any more of my dignity. If he wouldn't acknowledge me, then I refused to be the girl waiting around, hoping to change his mind.

Because I had a better plan! I showered and dolled myself up as much as I possibly could, given my lack of supplies. I put on the nicest thing I had with me: a green Billabong shirt and brown dress shorts. My hair was untamable. It'd been gelled into place with all the salt water and not showering. My face was also beyond sunburned, and I was disappointed that no amount of makeup could hide that fact, but I did my best to cover it up.

I packed up my tent and my guitar. My life fit neatly into the back of a hatchback once again. After deciphering the chicken-scratch map, I located the house. Upon my arrival, I was introduced to a guy who'd landed in New Zealand after studying at a university in Australia and never left. Everyone called him Texas.

My connection with Texas was too easy. Two Americans who'd studied abroad next door. We were both guitar players and very good Mexican joke tellers. (As a Mexican mutt, I'm allowed to tell Mexican jokes.) The thought crossed my mind: *That could be me. Maybe they'll call me Wisconsin.*

As I played Texas' guitar, everyone chatted about a barbeque that would take place that night. I brushed it off and helped prepare the vegetables. With my creepy stalker plan well underway, I was happy to assist.

When we drove over to the neighbor's house, we passed someone walking. Jack and Texas pointed him out because I didn't recognize him. A hooded grey sweatshirt, baggy shorts, and a baseball cap was quite the switch from the fitted uniform, red vest, ice axe, and boots Mason was wearing earlier that day.

Mason said hello, but then he avoided me for the next hour. Lucky for me, his confidence increased with each drink, as did mine, and that's when I took off the ring.

Grilled sausages were being handed out like popsicles. Ketchup dripped down my hand (with pre-vegetarian enthusiasm). Finally, Mason and I crossed paths and migrated to a nearby picnic table. After a few minutes, he made his move. When Mason poked at my hand and grabbed it underneath the table, I couldn't hide my smile. I was thrilled to receive even the smallest signal of approval.

I could sense significant territorial tension when an attractive, brown-haired, blue-eyed woman sat down across from us. Their history was implied. I could smell it, so I guzzled a few beers in attempt to ignore the situation. Wickedness clouded my mind, and Mason decided it was time to leave the party. Everyone hooted, hollered, and whistled as they witnessed our departure.

When Mason asked to take a walk with me, I agreed, knowing where the walk would lead to. It wasn't the first time a man was attempting to seduce me, and I let it happen. But the hours that followed were filled with regret.

Fox Glacier to Waikinae Beach
I felt disgustingly dirty. I'd never felt quite that horrible before because I knew very well what I was trading in, God for a night with a guy I liked. Mason had to work that day, so he

was out the door before I was dressed. I wanted to stay one more day to sort myself out, but I knew that if I stayed, I was putting myself at risk of never leaving. So I left that cabin with only a phone number, a last name, and absolutely no dignity.

I traveled 45 minutes before I pulled over to nap in the sun. I used my towel to block the light from my eyes. The feeling of a hangover was too familiar, the feeling I'd thought I'd forever abandoned. When I woke up, my head had cleared some, but my heart still ached. The beauty of my surroundings dulled some. The feeling reflected how disconnected I was from God.

I located a camp site next to Lake Hawea early in the day. I gazed at the mountains across the lake, assembled my tent, layered up for the evening, cooked my noodles, and fell asleep by 6 p.m. The shame was heavy.

I woke up early, but my conscience weighted me down and sent me crawling back into my sleeping bag. I grabbed my Bible, prayed, and read until I drifted off again. I slept half the day away, swimming in a sea of self-pity. But eventually, I showered, washed it off, and decided to move on.

The waterfalls I stopped at along the way diverted my attention away from myself and back to God. By the time I'd reached Wanaka, I'd sort of forgotten about Mason. I stumbled upon a café and ate outside on a bench. I soaked in some sun as I caught up on my journaling. Two men walked past me and offered to buy me a beer. I smiled passively. I took my time eating, somewhat intimidated by the invitation, afraid to let myself drink again.

I was caught as I attempted to walk past the pub unnoticed, so I took a gamble and stepped inside. My slow drinking pace prompted the entire bar to make fun of me, but I managed to hold my ground long enough for the group to become too drunk to notice my lack of drinking. I stayed because I'd connected with a couple of the girls, but one beer was enough to cloud my mind that night. My heart ached and in my desperation, I walked to the only pay phone in town to dial the barely legible numbers Mason had left me. When I didn't reach him, one of the locals offered me a couch to sleep on, and I found comfort in a warm place to stay and a free dinner.

I woke up early to avoid an awkward goodbye to bar friends I'd never see again. I couldn't sleep past the sunrise anyway, so I showered quietly and left a note on the counter. I was ready to be alone again.

I sang in the car, winding back and forth down the hills, tears streaming down too. At the bottom, I located an information hub and inquired about the infamous Queenstown bungy jump. Then I walked into a hostel with a laundry bag full of things for the night.

Three guys were playing cards in the lobby. Alex was from Chicago, which made him only the second American I'd seen in New Zealand. Talking with Alex reminded me of how fond I was of Mason. He was the fraternity boy of all fraternity boys. Most of the contributions he made to the conversation were drinking-related comments, and I was pretty repulsed by his recommendation to get drunk before my bungy jump.

In my loneliness, I turned on my phone for the first time in days and saw that I had a message from Mason. I was relieved to learn that he hadn't forgotten about me! I started engaging with the fantasy, and you never would've known that I was filled with remorse only a few days ago. The way we met could've been made into a movie. I was a broken girl from a small town on the other side of the world. And my ice climbing guide—the one with wavy hair, accent, and ice axe—liked *me*. Who wouldn't be tempted to get caught up in that kind of love story? I couldn't fall asleep that night, between the thoughts of my new romance and visualizing the 134-meter plunge I'd take the next morning.

I hopped on a computer at the A.J. Hackett Bungy Shop to distract myself from the thought of jumping. The bus ride to the jump site was an agonizing 45-minute ride, and even the sign on the bathroom door increased my adrenaline flow: a picture of a cartoon woman hanging upside down. The staff then swiftly fit me with a harness and requested a signature, one that supposedly signed my life away.

The walk to the wire, cage-like transporting mechanism was basically like walking the plank. Each of us was clipped to a bar in the center of the wire box before we made our way to the jumping base, just in case. As if the anticipation wasn't already too much to handle, we were then lined up by size and weight. I was slotted to jump second to last, meaning I had the privilege of watching eight people jump before me. Were they having the heavier men jump before the rest of us to test the rope? I wasn't sure, but I was sure that there was something about watching a grown, 200-pound man become hysterical before leaping from the platform that really made me nervous.

I've got a Feeling by the Black-Eyed Peas was blasting on the radio as I mentally prepared. Fortunately, I was able to sit as someone strapped me in and checked the carabineers. A quick flash let me know that my picture was being taken. I stared at the camera with bug eyes, unaware that my right hand was making a "rock on" hand gesture. Someone clutched the back of my harness as I stepped out onto the metal platform. He tapped me on the shoulder to get my attention, but a fog horn could've been sounding right next to my ear and I wouldn't have flinched. So he grabbed my chin and pointed my face towards the camera. Not my most attractive picture.

Then he counted for me. Five. Four. Three. Two.
One.

I jumped.

I dove chest first. I fell faster and faster and watched the river and the rocks come closer to my face. Then I bounced like a yo-yo a few times. I unstrapped my leg straps and allowed my body to sink farther into my harness as I was instructed. Then I was reeled up like a giant fish out of the water, slowly but surely. I swung and smacked the side of the jumping platform before three pairs of hands reached out to pull me up. I stepped onto the platform and heaved a massive, "Whew!" before asking if I could go again. The adrenaline high lasted the rest of the day, and I found comfort in learning to view my extravagant jumps out of planes and off platforms as being no different than allowing Jesus to have control over my life.

After returning to the hostel and eagerly sharing with Alex every detail of my jump, I accepted his invitation to hike up the Tiki Trail to the gondola summit. The walk up the trail was more intense than what I thought I'd signed up for, not just physically, but also emotionally. I'd passively mentioned my Bible study, which prompted non-stop questions to spew from Alex for the next three hours.

"What about sex before marriage? How is it even possible to accomplish that?" he asked.

"It's hard, I know. It's possible though. God only wants what's best for us," I said as I thought about my ring. Alex complemented me by telling me that I could be God's spokesperson, which was the most encouraging thing I could've heard right then. God clearly answered my prayer and gave me the words. On our way back to the hostel, we stopped at a deck and took a picture of ourselves in front of a large kiwi statue. My hair turned golden as the sun emerged from behind the clouds, a symbol of the conversation that was had.

I waited for the guys to leave the hostel before I took a deep breath and dialed. This time, Mason answered. It was as if we were in the sixth grade, what, with all the spontaneous giggling, awkward pauses, and roundabout ways of saying things. We agreed to meet in Christchurch.

The next morning, I jolted out of bed and rushed to pack my things, a notch below complete panic. The water I saw along the way was the bluest water, even bluer than the sky, enough to convince me that maybe my world really had been turned upside down. A city full of roundabouts and intense, angry traffic wasn't part of the plan. Nevertheless, I located the general vicinity of our meeting place with eagerness. While I anticipated his arrival, I concealed myself in the front seat of my car and read the final few pages of *My Sister's Keeper*. Luckily, I dried my tears before he arrived. Wouldn't that have been great? Mason showing up to find me all alone, blubbering like a little baby as I waited for him. No, thank you.

When Mason turned up, we awkwardly embraced each other. Were we friends? Were we dating? Did he care that we barely knew each other? I had so many questions that I didn't dare ask aloud, so I slipped on his sweatshirt, and we walked towards a pier in the outskirts of Christchurch. The wind forced us together. It also prevented us from saying anything.

We woke up early the following morning, packed our things, and headed north. My attention was diverted away from the beauty of my surroundings to the desires of my heart, desires to be known, loved, and free. After a picnic, we proceeded to the nearest playground and amused ourselves with the monkey bars and marry-go-rounds. In our New Zealand accents—mine well-rehearsed—we imitated Bear Grills and chased ducks through the tall grass.

"Crikey, there's a massive one!" My belly soon ached with laughter.

The ideas that followed were comparably brilliant. We mimicked statues while standing atop large, cement walls. Cars passed by and pointed at our embarrassing positions. Our boredom only led to more ridiculous choices. The grand finale of our evening included log rolling down a hill, which resulted in scraped legs and bruised arms. I was incredibly uplifted by our childish behavior. I felt like I could be my goofy self around him, yet the weight of my guilt suppressed that sense of freedom like a helium balloon ensnared in the trees.

Mason seemed so desperate for meaning, so eager for love. He confided in me that he wasn't sure what his life's purpose was. As I reclined next to him about to succumb to my body's need for rest, I reassured him, "Mason, your life doesn't have to be that way." Mason accepted me and praised my confidence in God, and he began to worship, just not in the way I wanted him to. I became the object of his adoration. And in that moment, I knew I'd never live up to his idea of me.

Mason and I took our time driving. We paused to rest in the sun for a few hours, my head on the sand and his on my belly. When we built a fire on the beach, I was lost in awe of God's amazingness. The sun was setting over the water, and I couldn't tell where the sky ended and the water began. Every romantic and dreamy moment that we shared together served to numb the guilt, and I kept telling myself that God wanted me to be happy.

The guilt resurfaced when we stopped at a Christian campground. The posters, signs, and personality types guaranteed it. I was more than aware that what I was doing—setting up a single tent with a man who wasn't my husband—

was wrong. I felt that all eyes were on me, observing my sin. But of course, no one said anything to me.

Waikinae Beach to Auckland

The following day Mason and I went on an eight-hour hike through the Tongariro Alpine Crossing, which is supposedly the greatest day hike in New Zealand. The base of the mountain was a perfect 70 degrees, yet when we approached the first volcano crater, we were engulfed in a blustery blizzard. The vivid white prevented us from seeing more than a few feet in front of us. And on the other side of the craters, volcanic ash made for a playful run down a steep hill to Blue Lake. The stench of sulfur — the smell of rotten eggs — motivated us to keep moving. Finally, a lush rainforest escorted us to the other side.

I missed God when I was with Mason. Mason seemed to be everything except one thing. Even so, I crumbled when he left. I whimpered as I tried to keep my face from scrunching up. We made plans to visit each other before engaging in a lengthy, dramatic goodbye. Honestly, I wasn't sure I'd ever see him again.

I ventured back to the campground where Mason and I had spent the night. I cried at the sight of it, so I decided to sleep at a hostel instead. An older woman greeted me at the door and welcomed me in as any grandmother would. She showed me every nook and cranny of her home, and I was cared for with a hot tea and shower.

I often didn't wear shoes in Australia. Feeling the ground against my feet forced me to be relaxed wherever I went. I walked to the supermarket and to the pay phone, my skin coming into contact with the dirt and grime. After saying goodbye to Mason, I took my shoes off and started to come back to myself. I even strolled in and out of the hostel barefoot, as if it was home.

As I pressed on, I felt more and more compelled to deviate from the mainstream routes. I turned onto Highway 45, also known as Surf Highway, and followed signs for a camp site. Around 20 kilometers of a remote stretch of road led me to an adorably wrinkled, grey-haired man passionately playing his guitar on his doorstep. I paid my camping fee, grabbed my guitar, and marched towards the giant, black sand dunes that lined the beach. I successfully made it past the kiwi birds that mocked me, and I was soon lost in a dream of creating music and appreciating the eloquence of the growing shadows on the beach.

The old man saw me with my guitar and invited me in. He showed me his music studio, offered me a copy of his cd, and shared of his many adventures with famous artists like Neil Diamond. My jaw dropped in admiration when he revealed more than 50 signed photographs of various celebrities. They were framed and neatly hanging on his once white walls. He told me to never stop playing, to never give up on my dreams.

I left the following morning, wishing I didn't have to. I worked my way up the coast of the North Island and stopped in New Plymouth where I rewarded my four weeks in a tent with a much-needed and well-deserved trip to a salon.

"I haven't showered in days, so I apologize if my hair is a bit ratty. I've been living in my tent."

"So you like, actually slept outside in a tent?" She asked, reminding me that I'm not that much of a girly girl. Immediately after I stepped outside, the clouds released their tension and the rain destroyed my freshly styled hair, but I still felt beautiful.

On my way to Auckland, I toured the Waitomo Caves.

When I peered up at the glow worms, I was deluded to believe I was outside in the dark of the night gazing up at the stars. I was surprised by how comfortable I was in the frightening and chilling atmosphere of the cave's shadows. I was sure that my breath was creating a cloud in front of me, but I couldn't see it. I hugged my knees while I sat in the boat and pondered what was ahead, but I wasn't afraid.

Entangled

WHEN I ENTERED THE OUTSKIRTS of Auckland, I drove around in search of a camping site but had no luck. Staying directly in the city wasn't my original plan, but I didn't mind the music, the sophisticated harbor, and the classy little restaurants. I sacrificed nine dollars (a lot of money at the time) to listen to a local band play Fat Freddy's Drop cover songs. The band also played some dated tunes in a reggae-like fashion. When I heard *When You Say Nothing at All*, I found myself blinking back a few unexpected tears. Was it the song? Was I really that tired?

I located a hostel downtown after dinner. It rested above a scandalous bar, and I deemed it dirty. I settled into my room with my head hung low. My roommates were discussing heading to a nearby strip club. Drugs were readily available next door. I perched myself on the top bunk and dangled my feet off the side. The ladies' gossip was like that of high school girls, and listening to it made me queasy. I wasn't ready to be shoved back into reality.

I'd yet to pack the car. I guess I was a bit distracted by all the irony, by Reality's insistence that it be acknowledged and heard. When I turned on the radio the morning before my flight, I heard: "If there's anyone you'd like to say happy birthday to, anyone at all on this fine day, please call now." I started laughing, slowly at first. My dad's birthday is the one day a year when I allow myself to have a look, open the door and feel the draft, mourn what never was, and acknowledge the desperate darkness of a man who I don't believe will ever come undone. His birthday isn't about sending him subliminal wishes or feeling sorry that he might be sitting there all alone. It's about me taking a day to remember, to feel. I think I owe it to myself, to remember what little bit of a dad I *did* have. And to accept the death of a dad who hasn't died.

It's the shortest day of the year where I live, and with each passing year, the role my father has played becomes an even smaller part of my life. A piece but not the whole. The start but not the end. As much as you'd think that these thoughts would leave me upset or angry or all the above, they didn't. They don't. And that's the scariest, most wonderful part of it all. In that moment, I knew that it was done for me and always would be. It was as if my father was a bird, and I'd carried him with me wherever I went. I'd even taken him with me all the way to Australia and to New Zealand, but in that moment, I opened up my hands and let him go.

I packed my things in a parking lot and paused at a café before heading to the airport. Birds had managed to make their way in, and they chirped joyfully. I sighed and read, "And if he finds it, truly I tell you, he is happier about that one sheep than about the ninety-nine that did not wander off" (Matthew 18:12-14). I was encouraged to know that God was overjoyed to have me back.

I said goodbye to my hatchback, Stella. I wanted to take her with me. After all, she'd been my home for a month. I spent many nights sleeping in that back seat, all curled up against my guitar case. But maybe home is not a place. Maybe home is with the people you leave your heart with when you go. And maybe, in some small way, New Zealand was my home because home is wherever God and I go together. Home was in the hatchback. Home was in Wisconsin with my family. Home was on the cold tile floor of the Auckland International Airport.

I knew that where I was going was more important than everywhere I'd been. But everything felt so…so normal when I returned to the states. Almost as if I'd never left.

I slept in the same room as my brother that night. It felt like we were kids again, a night of fun sleep, only without the barrier of our father between us. We talked like camp kids gossiping late into the night. I'd prayed for the right words, and they came without stuttering or hesitation. I shared my faith with him that night. He finally felt like my brother again, and I was so glad that years of avoiding awkward conversations about our father were finally over.

I crammed everything I owned into my car. Boxes and blankets pressed against the windows. I didn't have an apartment yet, but I made the journey back to Minneapolis trusting that I'd find one. No one knew me in Minneapolis. No one understood where I'd been. Only for once, I actually wished they did.

I attended a Christian conference my first weekend back. In one of the sessions, I saw a video about a young man visiting his dad in prison. In the clip, the son never spoke. He only held up cards with his words written on them. Each card further described what his father did to his mom, how his father sinned against him and his entire family. But then the last card read, "Father, I forgive you." I know I was meant to be at that conference, even if it was just to see that video.

James' phone number was one of the only numbers that I still had saved to my phone, so I called him. We enjoyed a cup of coffee as I shared all about my faith story and my time abroad. I was encouraged as I prayed that night that James would find God, but a busy American life began to drown out the previous six months. Faith, prayer, and letting go of my past was so easy when I was abroad, but at home, it was a fight. I couldn't seem to escape my feelings of guilt, not even by traveling 8,000 miles in the opposite direction.

I didn't exactly say no when Mason offered to visit me. At least I'd resolved to inform him of my decision to be pure (not have sex with him). I'd date him, goof around with him, sleep in the same bed as him, and not have sex. What a great plan! I was going to tell him that it was all a big mistake, a huge misunderstanding. I was going to take it all back and start over with this non-believing guy.

The initial confrontation went surprisingly smooth. We agreed—me eagerly and Mason rather reluctantly—to no longer embrace a physical relationship. I cleared the air. I told him about Jesus. Mason even started to shift from apathetic to curious. In my zeal, I gave him my *Case for Christ* book. It was a balancing act of convincing him to read the book but not pushing so hard that he'd run the other way, away from Jesus and away from me.

Throughout our time together, my inner turmoil morphed. My convictions were soon extracted. Like a yo-yo, one minute shame overwhelmed me, and the next I was getting into bed with him without a care in the world.

Two weeks later, I dropped Mason off at the airport before dawn. He'd arrived in Minnesota before I'd even solidified a place to live, so with him gone I was alone in my apartment for the very first time. I sprawled out as if I was about to make a snow angel on the carpet. I was caught up in the romance of my fancy love story, yet I was imprisoned by my actions.

Since I'd already treated Mason as if we were married, I convinced myself that I could never leave him. That was my way around the sin. I believed the lie and bound myself to him, told myself that I *had to* love him.

While we were apart (me in the states and him in New Zealand being the ultimate long-distance relationship), I searched for community and support. I set aside my anger and even invited James to attend a church service with me. James and I started over. As friends.

I saw the person I was before, and I wasn't sure I knew her anymore. In Australia, it seemed easy, but in Minneapolis, it felt as if I was in a never-ending competition with the world around me. I wasn't quite good enough, always a step behind. There was always one more assignment to do or accomplishment to be had. School overwhelmed me, and the college party atmosphere challenged me.

I seemed to be stepping back into the life of someone I didn't know anymore. I was slowly becoming her again. I still played my guitar, but not without a beer in front of me or a dip in my mouth. And no matter what I did, I couldn't seem to numb the pain of my obviously non-Christian relationship. The only thing that sort of helped was the fact that we were separated for a few months at a time.

Sin had complete jurisdiction over my life. I worked ungodly hours to succeed in school. To bed at two and up at six in the morning was not uncommon for me. And when my ability to focus would flee, I'd crawl into my bathtub and bawl. Once, a bath wasn't even drawn. I was fully clothed. I just sat there, wanting to hide, maybe even drown. I just didn't know where else to go. I lived alone. I didn't have a church, and I didn't have many friends.

I started hanging around a grad student. He showered me with fancy martinis, drinks that would leave any cheap college student in awe. He wooed me with his guitar. Sound familiar?

But who cares? It was my manipulation that was really the problem. Manipulating men had become a game to me.

In the depths of despair, doubt began to dawdle. I hated having doubts, but keeping faith in the middle of my sin, my aloneness, and my dying grandpa—it was too much. I left my apartment in the middle of the night and drove five hours to see my grandpa one last time. Right before he died, Grandpa said that he spotted little children playing on the floor in front of him. I like to think that they were angels guiding him.

Being in a long-distance relationship meant I had two lives. There was my Minneapolis life: my faith struggle and isolation while dabbling in depression. And there was my life with Mason. My life with Mason may have been a lie, but it was a beautiful lie.

Then one day I was waiting to board my third and final flight. Only two hours separated me from seeing Mason again. My eyes lingered over my shoulder as I walked. I saw the same bench I'd waited on only five months prior. I'd done it, actually wished myself back to New Zealand.

Lying in Mason's bed prompted flashbacks. The climb, the barbeque. Yet everything was a blur. I was far from myself. I walked on egg shells in fear that I'd screw something up. I'd yet to start work at the glacier guiding office, so I spent most of my days in the cabin alone, waiting for Mason to come home. I'd stare at the door in silence until it finally opened. Moreover, I was nothing but a torrent of negativity.

Why didn't I just get some air, go outside? Besides being just a tad depressed, I had no car to escape in. I was living in the middle of nowhere. I did bike through the mountains one day though. I fought through the hills and the trees to make it to the beach. When I saw the water, I let my bike crash beside me. Freedom. Finally. But like dinner fed to the dog while mom's in the kitchen, I hurried home so that Mason wouldn't even notice that I'd been gone.

In the process of unpacking and organizing my things, I uncovered one of Mason's old birthday cards in a cupboard. Naked women were plastered all over it. I was devastated, as if I'd been cheated on. That discovery led to a series of full-cabin searches for porn and love letters.

I felt most insecure at night, when I was alone and my thoughts could run wild. Why did I have hair on my skin? Why couldn't I be thinner? Why couldn't I be more like the images that I knew he'd seen? Maybe if I had a bigger this or smaller that? And even if he said he wasn't comparing me, how could I believe him? I started to wonder if maybe real love just didn't exist.

It was ironic that one of the most beautiful places in the world seemed so absent of God. I walked past that old, run-down, Catholic church every day. The windows were boarded up, and bugs consistently crept out of the cracks in the walls. But maybe I felt that way because there was so much sin thriving in my own heart, as if my insides were leaking out, sliming up my surroundings.

How was I trapped in New Zealand where I was once so free? I felt like crying all the time. I'd wished for Mason to go away long enough so I could. I felt like old news to him. Depression sucked the life out of me, which I hate admitting because I know how many people would give just about anything to spend that much time in place like New Zealand. Honestly, the only thing that kept my head above water was learning to snowboard while I was there.

Mason usually left me at the top of the chair lift so that he could ride with his more talented friends. I'd throw a fit when he'd leave me alone, but on some level, I cherished that time. I learned to love my board and being alone. I kept challenging myself to go faster, steeper, higher.

Saying bye to Mason was incredibly difficult because I'd yet to see the connections between my depression, my sin, his demeanor, and our relationship. I knew upfront that being with him would change me, and it had. I'd stopped going to church, reading my Bible, writing. I'd stopped everything.

Deep down, I think I knew that Mason and I couldn't be together. Our love was stimulated by beautiful places and not each other, and I couldn't follow him on his snowboarding adventures forever. I'd want a marriage and a family and a job one day. And we didn't believe in any of the same things, but I guess I wouldn't see it until I saw it.

Three months later, I boarded another plane to visit where he was staying at the time, a small town in Canada. When I arrived, I wondered why he didn't cook me dinner, buy me flowers, or even look at me as if I was worthy of being missed. I knew right then that our lives would never be the same. We'd never have the same values.

In my gloom, I wandered about the calm, quiet village. I was trapped in a winter wonderland, a human-sized snow globe. The lie that lived just beneath my skin festered. How was it that I could love someone so much, and yet want to run away from him with all my heart? I knew that I was in Canada to connect with God again but how? I wanted to go home.

In addition to snowboarding, I poured myself into running during my three-week stay in Canada. James emailed me: "If you can do eight miles, then you can totally run a half marathon!" His reassurance pushed me to register for my first half marathon. I was hopeful to know that I'd have something to look forward to, something to distract me from the pain when I got home.

New Year's Eve. An entire bottle of rum gone, no thanks to me. After Mason approached me, lifted my shirt, and forced me to flash a room-full at a holiday party, I insisted that we leave. We were forced to hitchhike our way home. A younger guy picked us up. I hopped into the back seat as Mason was ushered into the front.

Then the radio became stuck on a single channel. A song played that I knew, something I'd heard back at that conference. And for the first time in a long time, I felt a little poke, a signal from God. It was incredible, especially considering the situation I was in. Mason was in the front seat, soaring into oblivion, and I was all alone in the back, choking back tears. Why were those men blasting a Christian radio station anyway? But I guess they weren't. God was.

Mason could barely hold himself up, so I helped him into bed. He was rather irritated by my assistance. He pushed me and slammed the door in my face. Screamed that he hated me, that he wanted me to leave, so I did. Or started to. I packed my things. I'd seen enough. I'd finally seen what I'd needed to see.

I spent the next day applying for an engineering program that focused on improving the quality of health care in developing world hospitals. Focusing on something else helped ease the tension between my heart and my head. It was a little bit like planning my escape.

I hated that I wanted to be with him because I knew that I also wanted God. I needed God. I didn't want to need Mason. As I sat in the bathtub, alone and desperate, I read my Bible for the first time in over a year. That was the precise moment that I gave up, gave in. I couldn't live a double life anymore. Mason didn't know that we were saying goodbye forever in that airport, but I did.

I wasn't convinced that change was needed until I felt my

toes scrape along the bottom. Deception had gotten the best of me. I'd believed that I *had to* hit bottom. To be able to push off again, to be able to push hard enough to bring my head back above the water.

It'd been about a month since I decided to return to my faith, to God, to the kind of life I was being called to live. I endured a few shaming phone calls and manipulative pleas, but God kept me strong in my decision to leave Mason and my old life behind. Even after receiving a lengthy, hand-written apology from him, I knew to my core that I couldn't go back to that. Grace was abundant in many forms, including patience, courage, help, strength, and love when it wasn't deserved.

Buying a journal had always been a symbol of an attempt to start over. A new journal was an indication that there were things in my life I didn't want to remember: pain, decisions, reality. All of my journals remained only partially filled until I returned from Canada. For the first time ever, I penciled the final few words on the very last page. Then I went out and bought a new one. The right way.

Challenged

JAMES UNEXPECTEDLY TURNED UP AT my apartment only weeks later and confessed that he still had feelings for me. I had the sense that God brought him there, but I wasn't sure. Could I really trust myself after the decisions I'd made with Mason? So when James asked me out to dinner, I said no. Why would God bring someone else into my life who wasn't a believer? It made no sense.

When he offered to cook me dinner, I finally said yes, not realizing it was Valentine's Day. The atmosphere was safe and comfortable, partly because we were living in the same apartment building, and joining him upstairs seemed harmless. We didn't kiss, but when we hugged, my giddiness squished out.

I was torn. I was incredibly reluctant to date someone who didn't share my faith, but James was the most caring person I'd ever met. He was boldly different, far from the arrogant, jock type. He was a leader, a clever engineer, a cook, a marathoner. I could go on and on.

There was a part of me that didn't even want to go to church with James that day, but I knew that I needed to. The church was old and rustic, an established resident of downtown Minneapolis. After a message, music, and an encounter with God I wasn't even aware of, we parted ways. James called me soon after, to thank me. For what? Wheels spinning, energy spilling, James wanted to make his faith official. I told him that it was a gift he needed to accept, and I encouraged him to tell that to God in a prayer.

Over the next hour, I happened to find some writing from my time in Australia. I also just so happened to locate something I'd written about James, for James. It was a prayer for him to know Jesus. I was honored that God would choose me to help bring someone to Him. Never had I felt so genuinely happy for another person, and that was the last thing I needed to see in James. I knew I loved him right then.

If it weren't for James, I probably wouldn't have registered for the Twin Cities Marathon. My excitement was displayed in my smile and a bounce in my step. I spontaneously joined James in running a half marathon one weekend. I hadn't registered, but I ran anyway and dodged the finish line at the end. When I'd run, nothing could imprison me. That run brought my total up to 41 miles for the week, and I'd barely noticed the start of marathon training.

Running caught me off guard. It was almost as if I didn't choose running. It chose me. It hurt to keep going, but quitting was never an option. Running was everything my life wasn't.

In another run, I led a pack of eight men twice my age. "Unify our world. Our shoes are placed together in harmony. Rebirth of the sun. We are one" (*Rebirth of the Sun*). The music always pushed me to run faster. I finished alongside them. The men congratulated me.

When I wrote about that run later that night, I found a note tucked between the pages: "This is what I need: I need him to know me. I need him to accept me. I need him to support me. I need someone who knows Jesus." I'd written it down, so I could remind myself. And when I read over the words, I knew that the man I wanted in my life was James. I couldn't have been more sure.

I found flowers on my kitchen table one afternoon. James

was congratulating me on my acceptance into the engineering program. Another opportunity to travel was a dream come true, but I wasn't exactly excited about the idea of leaving James for two whole months. When I applied, I was eager to run away. But suddenly, I wasn't so sure I wanted to.

I was more wide-eyed than an owl at midnight when James grabbed me and kissed me for the first time in my kitchen. I'd never felt that kind of rush before. I let go of everything and let myself fall. I skipped nearly everywhere I went. And after a run one day, James asked me to listen to a song. Tucked within the lyrics were the words, "I love you." Was it true? Did he love me? We cuddled on my bed with my head on his chest, his arm around me. Two puzzle pieces. And I told him, "I love you. I want to marry you someday."

James and I savored the solitude during our hiking trip that spring. We went through it all together: the hot, the cold, the sun, and the rain. We hiked from sun up to sun down each day, flicking the ticks off our socks as we went. While wearing next to nothing, we huddled together to keep warm. Our clothes were drenched, the rain was relentless, and the early spring night was nearly freezing, but like innocent children, we seemed to be unaware of our near nakedness. Our tent collapsed. Our sleeping bags were completely soaked. It was worth it though, to kiss in the rain and be totally in love, James' words ringing in my ears: "You deserve it, Angel."

James was vastly different from every man I'd ever known. He was patient to date me, and he was humble in his pursuit of my heart. I was lost in a dream, forgetting where I was. We passed endless budding trees and lookouts. I caught a toad and scolded the squirrels for stealing my walnuts. I was a kid again. Innocent and pure. I kept thinking that I'd wake up at any moment, but I never did.

On our way to visit my family, we stopped at my aunt and uncle's house. I knew I wouldn't be asking my dad, and I think a part of me wanted my uncle's approval. Everything about my uncle reminded me of my dad. His mannerisms, his love for cooking, and his charm all reflected my father's only wonderful traits. Ironically, all things that James has too. My aunt winked at me from across the table as we enjoyed a late lunch together. "He's the one," I said with my eyes, and we giggled in our own little language.

A few days later, I prepared to leave for Costa Rica. My heart ached with unwillingness to go. Two months under the torture of having given James my heart and not knowing if he truly accepted it was less than ideal, but his flowers and letters would reassure me.

Another blurry whirlwind of sitting in an airport, waiting to board a plane. I already missed James as I sat in that airport, so I consoled myself by trying to think about how much I'd wanted another adventure. There was something so surreal about being there. It was somehow dreamlike and familiar at the same time. I was reminded of New Zealand and Australia. In fact, I'd sat on the very same bench before. I was lost in my reminiscent thoughts, unable to distinguish my real reason for being there until a man just a few feet away speaking Spanish jolted me back to my reality. I was about to hear nothing but Spanish. I was about to prepare to repair medical equipment at a hospital in Honduras.

It's times like that when I can feel God the most, when I'm all alone and at the mercy of God's will. That kind of trust is exactly what makes my relationship with Him flourish. As I got in line to board the plane, I was vaguely aware that I was about to learn something indescribable, seeing as James, comfort, money, and friends would be temporarily absent.

My host family didn't speak a word of English, and I had only enough time to greet my three roommates and settle into bed before the lights were shut off without warning, an indication that it was time we all stop whispering and get some rest. In the morning, I woke up to non-stop Spanish as if I'd been dreaming in Spanish all night.

On day one, we were warned not to be late to class unless we wanted to be sent home. We were also cautioned in our safety seminar that we'd most likely be robbed at some point, possibly at gun point. Supposedly the more horrible and scrubby you looked, the better off you were. I'd never experienced that in all my travels, the lack of freedom, the fear. Some adventure.

It was yet another typical college setting where most were focused on partying. I was the only one who wanted to get outside and run. To be safe about it, I was forced to lap the large hill right outside the host house door. Three minutes up. Three minutes down. Up. Down. Up. Down. It was repetitive and annoying, but at least it was something.

The training consisted of lectures, labs, and Spanish lessons. My inner engineer was giddy to be able to play with a multimeter and Ohm's Law. In lab, I constructed an extension cord. After class, we explored downtown. There was one brick street designated for pedestrians where people swarmed the streets like massive schools of fish. Fresh fruit stands, cute markets, and loads of specialty shops clouded the remaining space. It was sunny every morning and it rained every day, but the rain only lasted a couple of hours.

An alarm sounding at 4:30 a.m. was enough to make anyone grumble and stumble out of bed, but I was anxious to get out of the city. I left in the clothes I'd slept in, and past the dirty, busy city were huge, majestic mountains covered in lush green. Each mile traveled peeled away another cloud, revealing a further dimension of beauty. The bus snaked along the mountain-side roads for an hour before stopping for breakfast. I enjoyed a cup of coffee that was richer, bolder, and better than Starbucks on steroids.

Then the bus pulled over at the top of a long, gravel road. Our instructor, Gwen, invited us to run with her down to the river. Most decided to stay on the bus, but a few of us accepted the challenge. I felt quite crafty as I tied my sandals to my feet with shoe laces. I managed to run a whole mile in sandals and a bikini top for a bra, though it's not something I'd recommend. And it felt less than awesome to lather up the sunscreen over a thick layer of sweat.

To start, we glided through a few relaxed class one rapids. But the cliffs that stretched up high along the river sides made it impossible to escape what was ahead of us. Our guide, a quirky Jamaican man with a humorous flair, shrieked, "Get down!" as we began to combat the first sizeable rapid.

I ducked and I attempted to anchor myself by wedging my foot underneath the seat in front of me, but I still rocketed off the raft like a freshly popped piece of popcorn. I was swallowed by the river. I swallowed a bit of river too, and in my panic, my eyes bugged open. I tried to see through the murky, brown water until a hand stretched down and yanked me up by my life jacket.

Jamaica then pressured me to "ride the bull." I was urged to straddle the front of the raft and raise a hand in the air while screaming at the top of my lungs. A peculiar combination of courage and the need to redeem myself convinced me to accept the absurd challenge along with the inevitable outcome. I lasted 30 seconds before the river devoured me a second time. I was swept beneath the raft. Trapped for what felt like forever, but a pair of hands eventually peeled me out and threw me onto the raft. I'm sure that Jamaica no longer liked me at this point. I sucked at rafting, which made me a huge liability.

Someone hired a sports photographer for our trip, and I remember the guy photographing our picnic. There's this picture of me in my bikini top glaring at the camera man as if the photographer had just keyed the side of my car. The guys in the group all found this photo to be hilarious, but I hadn't agreed to "pose" in my swimsuit for him and I guess it struck a nerve.

Towards the end of the trip, I followed Jamaica to the top of a cliff. I hurdled myself off the edge and plummeted into the water below to reclaim my competence and reprimand all fear. I rested in my life jacket and allowed it to carry me. I floated about a mile down the river and ultimately landed in a pool of calm, shallow water where I enjoyed the serenity of the river's end.

In his first letter to me, James wrote, "I don't know how to describe it, but even though we're so far away, I feel close to you. Through prayer, I will always be with you no matter where you are." And I knew we were going to be okay.

I was getting bored with my morning hill circuit, so I decided to go for a real run the following morning. Exiting the house was my first project. I struggled with each of the doors, a series of bars and locks that tucked us in at night. My host mom had given me several unlabeled keys, and each door was secured with two separate locks. After escaping, I ventured up, hypnotized by the false sense of security that the early morning tranquility delivered. The empty streets gave rise to a completely different world, one absent of fear. I kept running up, towards the mountains. And on my way back down, I let gravity do all the work.

I'd become lost in the charm of the sun waking up over the mountains. I was way down the rabbit hole, completely clueless, no idea where I was. The cat calls and rude remarks sent me soaring in the other direction. I no longer recognized any of the buildings or street names. Up and down the hills. I was so stupid lost I asked a police officer where I could find the yellow supermarket—the only landmark I could think of. But he seemed to be just as confused as I was, probably because I'd asked them "in Spanish" if he'd seen an orange peel on the sidewalk. Water started wetting my cheeks as I pleaded with an old woman for help. My panic came to a head when I realized that being late to class would get me kicked out of the program. I did make it home eventually, but not before completing an accidental 12-mile run.

During the lab session that day, I constructed a variable power supply, and a stressful day of electrical risk taking was rewarded with group salsa lessons. Uncoordinated men outnumbered those that were suave. What do you picture when you think of a dude who enjoys circuit building, math, and fixing things? But the men were kind, and dancing with them made me think of James. I pictured us dancing in perfect, synchronized harmony. I was eager to hear his voice and tell him how much I loved him that night.

A conversation with Craig, a fellow student, quickly led to flattery. He asked me about my travels and all the crazy things I'd done. Craig's chatter was charming, his fawning flirtatious. I was so amazing! But I was also so very smitten with James.

The following weekend, we all boarded a bus to Monte Verde. The green was enthralling. All the creatures—from the creepy caterpillars to the cheeky monkeys—were so intricate and unburdened. There was a great deal of peace that could've been experienced in that rainforest, but the group was slightly obnoxious. At least I was reminded of my hike with James. The dark clouds poured forth a sense of euphoria. I giggled each time the group paused to catch their breath because James and I were warriors of the woods! We never stopped. The harder it got, the more we insisted that we press on.

In the morning, I threw on yoga pants and a baggy t-shirt and planted myself on the curb outside among the group. Any expectations that I managed to muster up during the bus ride were greatly exceeded when I pranced along the path to the first zip line tower. Dense fog lingered near the tree tops...

When I was little, my dad used to sing, "Rock a bye Kara, on the tree top. When the wind blows, the cradle will rock." Sometimes he'd say, "Rock a bye Kara, on the *tractor* top..."

"No daddy! That's not right. It's supposed to say *tree* top!" I'd squeal.

And down will come baby, cradle and all.

We lined up and waited to climb the 20 slippery, metal steps to the first zip line. My harness, helmet, and gloves didn't weigh me down, though they did make me look like a construction worker. A tunnel was created by the surrounding trees, but the dense fog prevented me from being able to comfortably view the landing platform on the other side. I was clipped in, the carabineer secured.

The hum of the zip line escalated in pitch as I glided faster. The intensity of the wind caused my hair to shoot straight back. Birds coasted alongside me. I slowed down by increasing my grip on the line behind me and slammed onto the platform where I was unclipped and sent on my way. I was all alone as I walked to the next platform. I inhaled the fresh, crisp air deep, eager for the time alone.

When I arrived at the final zip line, the longest and highest of them all, I paired up with the largest and spunkiest man of the group. I'd assumed that our combined weight would allow us to zip the faster. I was right. Luckily, my only responsibility was to hang on tight as we accelerated fast enough for my eyes to water.

The final challenge was daunting. The Tarzan Swing was a free fall followed by considerable amounts of swinging and screaming. The rain picked up just as I stepped onto the platform. I was the only one who didn't scream, probably because I was the most scared. But I covered my fear with unstoppable laughter as I swung back and forth. Rock a bye Kara, on the tree top.

The swing from the weekend to classes on Monday morning sure was a dramatic one. The weekdays were notorious for dampening my spirits. The buildings and garbage drown out the beauty of the mountains. I missed James. I was fearful of theft. The homework bummed me out. Running had morphed into a safety concern. And I longed for a hot bath, a cool day, a church service.

Gwen opened her home up to us. She provided us with a few grandma-caliber snacks along with wine and beer, but the classy get-together soon mutated into a full-blown frat party. As I waited for the party to end, I situated myself on the floor and sulked in my guilt from having shot gunned a beer with Craig. I stared at my toes, laced my fingers together, and let out all my air. *Still a pushover for attention and approval.*

Another engineer sat down next to me: "Why aren't you out on the dance floor like everyone else?" Because I didn't want to dance like *that*. I nodded towards the grinding as I defended my position on the floor. He got it. He was the first of eight students I discovered who was also a believer. We were able to organize a gathering where we each shared our experiences and faith, and with each acknowledgement of God I was refreshed.

I was assigned to present (in Spanish) on electrosurgery units, and I wasn't at all excited about it. I wasn't exactly fond of public speaking, especially when done in a foreign language on a technical topic. But somehow, I didn't stumble. I also managed to answer close to 30 follow-up questions. Gwen even complimented me on my pronunciation. My spirits were lifted with each assignment that I completed and each day that passed because I just wanted to leave, move on to Honduras, and go home.

I counted the days until I could see James again. A part of me was afraid to lose him. Thinking that maybe distance and time would change his mind, I was eager to return to him and reassure him. The letters were the only thing that kept my mind from turning everything upside down: "It all seems like a beautiful dream, a plan and story nobody on earth could've made up for us. You are special beyond what you can comprehend, and I see it in your eyes—I see glimpses of heaven," James wrote to me.

During my last run in Costa Rica, a pack of people swept me up. I started to race with them, unsure of where we were going or how far we were running. The expressions of spectators increased my adrenaline. *Why is she out there running with those men?* We turned a large corner and with the finish line in sight, our pace quickened. I completed my final strides with my hands held high. Music played as the flooded bleachers roared. I wiped the sweat from my face. I lied and told the guys at the finish line that I'd lost my bib. Apparently, my Spanish was improving because I received a medal for finishing the 10k race.

Feeling less than prepared for my mission in Honduras, I

hoisted my luggage up the stairs of the bus. Passengers stared at me as if I was carrying a bunch of makeup and fancy outfits. I was tempted to open it up and show of my scrubs, soldering irons, and screw drivers. Saying goodbye to Costa Rica was simple though. I was energized even though I knew it'd be another month before I was home.

My lack of sleep was evidenced by the gloss in my eyes. When we reached our host home in Honduras, my partner, Kate, and I were ecstatic to learn that we'd get to sleep in our very own beds. No more bunk beds. We set our alarm and sunk into the bliss of some much-needed sleep.

The next morning, we laced up as the sun began illuminating the mountains and long grass. The clouds were painted pink. The heat and humidity never rested. Even running at 5 a.m. couldn't keep me from sweating more than an entire football team, but I wasn't focused on that. I'd seen men carrying machetes, and they went about their business much too casually for my comfort. I was glad that Kate wanted to go with because I would've been too scared to go alone.

When we returned from our run, we confronted the first of many awkward mornings. The village didn't have running water. A lonely toilet and a bucket for bathing resided in our bedroom apart from the privacy of a door.

A loud honk was our signal to leave for work. I was alarmed by how quickly our presence was requested in the surgical unit. Scrubs were our magic weapon. They granted us access to each of the hospital wards.

In the afternoon, we met the hospital director and team of surgeons. The principal surgeons, nurses, and directors of each ward gawked at us in anticipation of a brilliant introduction. We were about as impressive as a couple of new-hires barging into the CEO's office, but faces lit up when we shared that we were hoping to repair the infant incubator within the first week. The director, however, folded her arms and pinched her lips without blinking as if to say, "Prove it." In doing so, she provoked Kate and I to obstinacy. We refused to leave the hospital without delivering on our promise.

During the weekend, Kate and I ventured to the beach. The sun was stronger than a swig of whiskey. Even the water was breathtakingly warm, but when sharp pains began to penetrate my foot, I darted out. The sensation was unique, comparable to the sting of a stingray, yet a stringy slime concealed my foot and leg. Jellyfish tentacles. The venom surged throughout my body, triggering shakes, tingling, and nausea. But before I could even think to pee on myself, two burly men approached us. My heart sank into my stomach when our eyes met. Something wasn't right.

The light of the sun reflected off the metal and into my eyes. The sight of that knife stole my breath. A tall, boney man commanded us both to sit down. I strained to comprehend the Spanish because his Honduran dialect was fast and muddled. All I could decipher was the word "assault." And all I could think was, *I don't think I need to be told that I'm being assaulted.*

As we helplessly sat there in our swim suits, the knife warned us not to move while our bags were searched. They took everything, including my camera, phone, and the running medal I had clipped to my key chain. As the tall man fumbled with my camera, I pleaded with him. I begged him to let me to keep the memory card that contained all my precious pictures. His nerves and anger heightened when no money was found.

He raised the knife.

Reaching my hand out only kindled more anger. His voice quivered when he yelled. We knelt in the sand, defenseless.

"I'm sorry. Take it," I sobbed.

I kept my eyes on the sand until the men finally departed with our things. We waited until their figures began to fade in the distance before we booked it down the gravel road on which we came. We mercifully stumbled upon a cab parked in a narrow driveway, the home of a driver. I hugged my knees to my chest and sat in silence during the ride home. I was so eager to remember what it felt like to be home, safe, and near James.

The experience kept us confined to our room for a few hours. We kicked our feet up, ate mangoes, and talked about everything. I told Kate about my dad. She asked me if I'd forgiven him, which caused the floodgates to open. I told her about my faith. Like flowers that spring up from vulgar pile of manure, much fruit came from us getting robbed at knifepoint on that beach.

That afternoon, I hailed a cab and hauled my emotions to a Wendy's in search of a reliable internet connection. I set up camp near an outlet and booted up my computer. I could feel eyes on me as if I was being stalked like prey. Fortunately, Skype came to the rescue. Talking to James and my mom calmed me. I continuously scanned the room as I told them what happened. I caressed the screen and tried to teleport myself home. I left when it didn't work.

On my way out, a little Honduran girl asked me if I was going to have a baby. I knew I was brilliantly bloated, and I already felt fat. Hearing this from a six-year-old didn't help. And what if she was right?

I flagged down the first taxi I saw and darted inside. A torrential downpour was flooding the streets, which caused me to lose a shoe in the gutter. Directions spit out of me in a murmur. The short, husky cab driver nodded in acceptance of my request. I had a long list of reasons to be hypervigilant at that point, starting with my dad and ending with that knife. So when he stopped the car unexpectedly, I hurriedly memorized the numbers posted on his dashboard.

I struggled to fall asleep that night. I snuck out of our room and called James from the landline. Talking about getting married lifted me up, but the idea of waiting until marriage to have sex tore me up inside. He didn't want me? I was confused and a little offended. And then the phone cut out. Uneasiness boiled and bubbled up through my heart. I had the strongest, inexplicable suspicion that I was being cheated on and yet…everything was fine. He called me right back right away: "I love you. I can't wait to be with you again."

Kate and I set out to find a post office one afternoon, which ended up being a window between two brick walls. The attendant accepted our money and tucked it into a metal cash box. A two-hour trip by foot, one hand-made envelope, a roll of duct tape, and several love scribbles later, my mission was accomplished: My love was sent.

Normally, I wouldn't be so easily lured into a mall. The advertisements, expensive clothes, large crowds. But I didn't have a choice. I couldn't conceal my embarrassment when I requested a single test from the pharmacist behind the counter. I didn't wait for my warranted change or receipt. With the test under my shirt, I bolted to the nearest restroom. I waited as the liquid slowly creeped along, eventually revealing a single line. No baby. Just stress.

I was so preoccupied with James and going home that I wasn't thinking much about my work or my weekends in Honduras. My hands managed to execute the actions, and my mouth proficiently said the words, but my heart was absent. I didn't care if I didn't go anywhere. I only went with Kate wherever she went because I couldn't stand being alone.

San Pedro Sula is supposedly one of the more dangerous cities in Honduras, so I was relieved when we passed through it quickly to reach Baja Mar. The people all gawked at us. We were the only people on board with fare skin. The bus was old and worn, and it wobbled as we journeyed down an old dirt road. I stared out the window, my eyes glazed over. I saw women with babies in their arms, baskets on their shoulders, washing clothes in large tubs while livestock aimlessly wandered amongst them. Boys paired up on rusty, old bikes. The community was more remote than anything I'd ever seen. Our hostel was nothing more than a cot and a cold shower, which was a sort of upgrade since I hadn't washed my hair in over a month.

Fortunately, I didn't personally witness the blood bath that took place right outside of our host house shortly after that. Someone was shot and killed in the middle of the afternoon. God comforted me though. My shoulders dropped down from my ears, and my breathing slowed. I closed my eyes momentarily to demonstrate my lack of fear. I planted myself in a chair and slurped on my ice cream shake. Time spent with God in the strangest of places, like at a Wendy's, came instinctively and naturally. I hated my time in Honduras, but I never lost hope.

I woke up to the tail end of a Miami weather update. The flight attendants were being summoned to their seats to prepare for landing. I'd originally planned to spend the night in Miami before heading home, but by that point, I couldn't bear the thought of it, so I pleaded with the airline staff.

"No, you don't understand. I have no money. I've been robbed! I have nothing left. I'm done. Please, I'm begging you. Can you put me on a standby flight? I just need to go home." It worked, probably because I started crying. I got to go home a day early.

From the very top of the escalator I could see James. He was standing on the tips of his toes, panning the people his eyes connected with mine. I raced down the moving steps and engulfed him with my limbs in a full-blown "monkey hug." Then we drove away from the airport. We were both beaming, squeezing our hands together so tight they hurt.

Those two months meant everything for our relationship. I didn't want them to happen, but they needed to. James and I both needed to be on our own in our faith, before we could be together in it. It was painful and completely worth it. We pressed our foreheads together until the sun came up. And before anyone came downstairs, he asked me to marry him.

Triggered

> "Reality is merely an illusion,
> albeit a very persistent one."
> – Albert Einstein

THE FIRST FEW HOURS OF our engagement were filled with a festive announcement, sparkling grape juice, cake, and congratulating comments. This was our "honeymoon phase," a whopping 48 hours. We struggled with our physical boundaries when we first got engaged, among other things. But we wanted our engagement to mean something, so we resolved to wait until we were married to have sex. And without that tool, I began to realize just how severely my security was enmeshed in sexual performances and physical reassurances.

James was neck-deep in his own battle with sin, enough to make my heart pound in my throat as the pain tried to escape my chest. Like a time traveler, I was propelled back—wrists bound, body bare, heart exposed. It was as if his actions woke me up to the memories of my dad and everything he'd done to me. Eugene Peterson once said, "Memory…is vigorously present tense, selecting out of the storehouse of the past, retrieving and arranging images and insights, and then hammering them together for use in the present moment." I was waking up from a dream, one I'd thought was true. That bottom stair I expected to be there wasn't. It was difficult to regain my balance. What was wrong with me? I was insecure. Numb. And even though I'd experienced heartache before, I found myself feeling more broken than ever.

If I couldn't even believe God, how was I going to believe James? I'd stare and compare. I'd hesitate to introduce James to my friends out of fear. I searched, thought that maybe Google would educate me on my rivals. How would I ever win? I wanted to barf. The messages. The figure I was supposed to have. The hair and makeup I needed to tolerate. The skin that had to be waxed. My insecurity was displayed as one big attempt to measure up to these "standards." Self-sabotage? Yep. I was an elegant piece of china that God had created, and I was essentially throwing myself against the sidewalk. I was shattering.

Agreeing to marry James thrilled me. And agreeing to marry James terrified me.

It triggered me. Like a disease. But we couldn't escape the world, not unless we were going to live in a tent on a mountain top in the middle of absolutely nowhere (which by the way, I would've been perfectly fine with). One time, we were stopped at a red light, and an image of a woman posing seductively in nothing but a pair of mesh tights was on the back of the city bus right in front of us. The greatest irony of all: This was an ad for *clothes*. The point is: I couldn't run from her. And I couldn't beat her.

I demanded to be present at all times—at a social event, a run around the lake, a trip to the store—because paranoia was my daily decree. My hatred for the heels slapping against the sidewalks was obvious. In clusters, they'd gather, like teams ready to rage against me. "Why are you doing this?" I'd ask myself. "I'm not doing anything!" I'd respond. I was justifiably angry. It wasn't me. It was my history.

I'd imagined that obtaining beauty and disregarding my feelings would somehow give rise to security. All the while, I longed to hear God's approving words for me: "I created Kara exactly how I want her to be. I know Kara." And yet every time I heard the word "beautiful," I'd cringe. Because I didn't believe it. I wouldn't receive it.

I fought the urge to earn my worth. I dabbled in the realm of every extreme. I ultimately eliminated everything (alcohol, coffee, even beauty routines) in an effort to gain the love and acceptance that I so deeply desired. But Philip Yancey writes, "The solution to sin is not to impose an ever-stricter code of behavior. It is to know God."7

Then one night I pulled my eye lids forward and carefully sketched on my face. I concealed my flaws. Enhanced my features. Though mid-April in the Midwest, it was raining, sort of snowing. I couldn't tell. I was frigidly cold and utterly uncomfortable for the sake of a hot outfit: fabric flats and barely-there t-shirt. Then I ordered a beer from the bar and started panning the room. Out on the dance floor, but my personal bubble shrunk until it popped.

One stuck out. Skinny and miniature…like the little girl I never got to be. Her hair stretched all the way down to her bouncing butt. Her tank top sat well-above her belly button, unlike mine that was tucked in. Why did she bother me so much?

Everyone was dancing but me. I was standing in the center—the eye of a hurricane—observing. Bodies pressed up against mine. I was okay with the goofy looking boys that bobbed their heads around me, but a trip to the ladies' room was all it took to remind me of the competition within that place.

Snap.

Heels.

Short skirts.

Primping.

Shot.

I wanted to run, but I had nowhere to go. I told James that I wanted to leave. I couldn't be there. I wasn't ready to face my triggers, but I saw disappointment in his eyes. He wanted to stay, and I wished I was better for him.

I squirmed through the crowd and made a bee line for the bathroom. I closed the door. The louder I sobbed, the more silent I felt. And when I twisted back through the crowd, I couldn't find James. I climbed the stairs and draped myself over the railing. Another girl was next to me. And another. And another.

Snap.

Tight shirts and cleavage.

Body-hugging pants.

Long hair and makeup.

And perfection.

Shot.

That's when I decided to get a cab. When it pulled into our driveway, I saw his car. He…he left me? I was angry. A rapid downward spiral where all negativity seemed to collide all at once within me. I reacted to all my pain, some of it true, most of it not.

"You left me!" I screamed, but he'd only left to find me. Everything within me wanted to be convinced that he was the one who'd abandoned me, so I'd have an excuse to run away. To flee and protect myself, to be alone and finally be released from my body defining me. I fired my words. I aimed well. They hit. They stung. In her novel, *A Visit from the Goon Squad*, Jennifer Egan writes, "Her only thought was of getting away, as if she were carrying a live grenade from inside the house, so that when it exploded, it would destroy just herself."[8]

At the end of the night, I needed his kisses to tell me that I was loved. I needed the same physical connection I'd always needed in order to know my worth. It worked. Sure, I fell asleep feeling secure, but I woke up under the weight of my manipulation with shame stamped on the inside of my wrist.

What race was I trying to win? What prize was I hoping to attain? Was it beauty? Love? Freedom from the pain?

That morning, I saw myself for who I really was: an addict dealing with the aftermath. Beauty was my nicotine, my crack, my cocaine. Beauty was my alcohol, what I used to excuse or ease the pain. And I was hungover from a horrible relapse where I let it control me, maybe even define me.

I waited for the queue, but the lights, they never went down. The momentary relief that I was prepared to feel arose from faith in the beauty of my body, not real security. I'd become confident in the costume I had on, but conditional security isn't really security at all.

I loitered around James like a lost puppy. I squeezed him. Assured him of my love. He told me it was okay.

"Is it?" I asked.

"It's in the past now," he assured me, but to me it was all the same. It *was* like a hangover. My stomach believed I was sick. My head was spinning.

As much as my past had inevitably hurt and changed me, I knew that if I continued to let it define me, I'd drown indefinitely. I'd ruin things. What was it to gain the world and lose absolutely everything else? Friends. My relationship with James. My relationship with God.

Snap. I saw his face. Daddy. Then he took a step back. He left. Was he ever really there? Shot.

My trigger. Evidenced by my race to be perfect, to be beautiful, to be loved.

I like to think of it as a spark, something that initiates the spreading of a forest fire throughout an entire day. Because for a moment, I couldn't tell if I was here or there, if I was me or her. I had no sense of reality. I'd mistaken a memory for the current minute.

How was I supposed to get rid of the masquerading memories that came with a swift smell? I couldn't will the cognitive mechanism to stop. *Try harder and it will all go away. Pray harder and it will all go away. Believe harder and it will all go away.* No! The moment that scent entered my airway, it was no longer a choice. The memory would come no matter how unwelcome it was, perhaps so rapidly and so frequently that my remembrances were organized into a "present folder" without my consent.

What was I supposed to do when every time I went to smell the roses, I was thrown back, with my wrists tied and my insecurities exposed? The roses weren't always at fault. When carefully handled, roses are exquisite and wonderful! But if the roses weren't liable, then I must've been, for what kind of woman thinks she whiffs rotten eggs when she has a face full of roses?

Or think of it this way: Consider a time when you coincidentally became sick after eating a certain kind of food. Sure, for a while you may refuse to consume what seemed to be the cause of your nausea. For a while, that food you upchucked gives you a good reason not to return to it, but chances are there will come a time when you're no longer proclaiming the pungency of that puked-up dinner. Eventually, your sickness is stored in your brain in the appropriate spot. Or is it possible to loathe your once-favorite food for the rest of your life due to *one* negative experience? Two negative experiences? What about three? How about a thousand?

There's a chirp that will always take me back: A high pitched squeal followed by a lower, much calmer whistle. One high and one low. When I close my eyes, a gentle breeze sways the trees, and I'm standing in the backyard that used to seem endless to me. This reverberation was my soundtrack when raking leaves, playing on the swings, and contemplating. His head has a prominent black cap and bib, the rest of him white. Chickadees make a time traveler out of me.

What happened throughout my life has harmed me, but more importantly, my past changed what I believed about God and the world. Some changes in my belief system were necessary because they protected me. They guarded me in a responsible way. But some changes were completely irrational. I was crazy to think that James was actually acting out the senseless gossip in my head.

I'd become comfortable being bonded to the lies my past conditioned me to believe. It wasn't an accident that my mom sent me to college with a children's book called *I Love You So...*, a story intended to reassure a young child that she's loved unconditionally. I needed to be reminded then. Sometimes I still do.

Each of these modifications in my belief system traced back to the stories that were told to me. Most women are insecure on some level, but I know plenty of women who actually believe their husbands when they tell them they're pretty. There are plenty who trust that their Christian men will still love them at the end of the day, no matter what. But more importantly, there are plenty of women who truly believe in God's love. At the time, I didn't believe. Maybe it'd been there all along, but that's when I started to notice the pain. A dull, persistent throb.

Was I ecstatic to be marrying the man that I loved? Of

course. But what was even more emotional was the fact that I wasn't simply saying yes to James. I was shouting yes to God. Getting married meant trusting God with my most severe fear.

And God was faithful. He began placing in me the purity I never had. As difficult as it was, I needed that interlude of reprieve where I wasn't warring with my worth through sexual performances. I needed James to listen to God. I needed James to help bring me back.

God chose James as a vessel to pour innocence back into me. The moment I started to recognize it, I was crying over a pumpkin. My hair was messy in a bun on the very top of my head. It was so harmless, so pure. In carving that pumpkin, I was beginning to be reunited with the child I used to be. Our bike rides were also childlike and precious. One afternoon, I dismounted, leaned my bike against the railing, and turned around to see James down on one knee, presenting me with a ring. I proudly placed the ring on my finger. I wanted the world to know.

James was my first New Year's kiss. He was also my first Valentine's Day date. Shocking, I know. After all those guys, there was so much I hadn't experienced. While I've given myself to many men physically, I've only ever prayed with one man.

I had no idea, but I'd been comfortably sailing above the mother of all icebergs, without a clue as to what lay beneath. The words of John Eldredge remind me of my own experience:

Once upon a time there lived a sea lion who had lost the sea. He had lived in a country known as the barren lands. High on a plateau far from any coast, it was a place so dry and dusty that it could only be called a desert. A kind of coarse grass grew in patches here and there, and a few trees were scattered across the horizon. But mostly, it was dust. And sometimes wind, which together make one very thirsty. Of course, it must seem strange to you that such a beautiful creature should wind up in a desert at all. He was, mind you, a sea lion. But things like this do happen. How the sea lion came to barren lands, no one could remember. It all seemed so very long ago. So long, in fact, it appeared as though he had always been there. Not that he belonged in such an arid place. How could that be? He was, after all, a sea lion. But as you know, once you have lived so long in a certain spot, no matter how odd, you come to think of it as home.[8]

It was normal for me to let my sexuality define me. It was all I'd ever known. But when James and I got engaged, the tip of that iceberg broke through the surface of the water, and the exposing of that iceberg began to mend the madness, to heal the shame, suffering, and soreness of my past.

Wedded

THAT OCTOBER, JAMES TUCKED ME in, said a prayer over me, and turned out the lights. I savored the innocence of that evening as I tried to remember that I wasn't a ten-year-old girl at a slumber party. Like a surefire formula for success, my gear and belongings were organized optimally. My shorts and muscle shirt were neatly placed on the floor. My bib was precisely pinned. My shoes, socks, watch, iPod, Advil, water bottle, and gel packs were carefully placed in a row.

I giggled as an original song replayed in my head. To prepare for the marathon, I'd eaten two whole potatoes as if they were ice cream cones and then giddily sang a song about it to the *Twelve Days of Christmas* melody.

The morning of the marathon was a blur. After three sips of water, two bites of cereal, and one cup of coffee, we were on our way. My heart started racing well before I did. James dropped me off near the starting point where the line for the porta potty wrapped around the block, and I made my way through my corral until I couldn't get any closer to the starting line. The crowd consumed me. They jumped nervously as their shoulders pressed against mine. Loud outfits, marked up legs, and decorated faces. Then the sound of the gun.

James had coached me to run painfully slow for the first five miles, but the adrenaline was too much for me. My pace increased at the start of mile four. As I ran past my niece at mile 13, the wind from my movement caused her hair to flow up and away from her face. At mile 20, my knee started to hurt, but I ignored it. Miles 21 and 22, I followed a runner with a verse printed on his jersey: "I can do all things through Christ who strengthens me" (Philippians 4:13). Mile 25, I couldn't feel my legs, so I poured Gatorade all over them and tried to slap a bit of life back into them. I was running uphill, breathing through the pain, the joy overwhelming. By mile 26, my body was overcome with chills.

The final stretch, I flew. I could see the capital building in the distance. My pace quickened. The crowd roared. I pumped my arms and finally lifted them up as I crossed the finish line in 3:46:00, only 11 stupid minutes shy of a Boston qualifying time. I claimed by bottle of chocolate muscle milk and proudly slipped on my finisher shirt. I felt like a warrior as I walked to the car, united with the other runners through pain. We all understood and supported one another. We all wanted it the same. We all hurt along the way, and there was no escaping the pain.

That December, my heart was making my shirt quiver as I dried my sweaty palms on my gym shorts. I could see through the cracks of the closed door that everyone else was dressed in normal winter clothes. When the door swung open, I was still hidden. Tears formulated inside but didn't come out. The song started to play just as I was summoned onto the stage: "In the shadow of the glorious cross..." I could see tons of people out of the corner of my eye, but I didn't turn to look at them. I was unashamed as I took a few steps forward, my skinny runner legs exposed, the light so bright. I stepped into the water and down the steps. My pastor then put his hand on my back and asked me a few questions. I nodded and grinned. I stepped forward, his hand on my shoulder.

The song ended only seconds before he spoke: "Kara, do

you now trust in Jesus Christ alone as your savior, for the forgiveness of all of your sins, for the fulfillment of all His promises that you will have eternal life?"

"Yes."

"Is it your intent, with God's help, to follow Jesus as Lord and obey His teachings?"

"Yes."

He turned me towards the congregation, toward all their bright, beaming faces. "Kara, upon your profession of faith, I now baptize you in the name of the Father, and of the Son, and of the Holy Spirit," he shouted.

He took my wrist and gently lowered me down and back up again. The congregation cheered as I wiped the water from my eyes and warmly wrapped my arms around my pastor. Then I walked back to the hall, drenching the floor along the way. I hugged James before he stepped out onto the stage. James and I were both baptized in the name of the Father, the Son, and the Holy Spirit in front of our church. I publicly proclaimed my faith in Jesus, and I trusted a man old enough to be my father to hug me, lower me into the water, and to bring me back up again.

That following May, I couldn't sleep, and when I sat up, my butt smacked against the ground. Sleeping on an air mattress was far from ideal, but James and I had agreed that I wouldn't sleep in our bed until after the wedding. I was still blinking back remnants of sleep: swollen lids, tired eyes. I was exhausted but too giddy to care. I scooped a spoonful of oatmeal into my mouth while I meticulously shaved my legs. Then I threw on a baggy shirt and sandals because someone else was going to do the rest of my getting ready for me.

I jotted down a few sentences in my journal and signed my new name, Mrs. Kara Rodriguez, before heading out the door. I cautiously carried my white, princess gown down the steps and out to the car. I tucked in the long, wavy end. The drive to the salon was quicker than I'd imagined it to be, so I took my time walking inside. Perfect waves framed my face. Purple and blue flowers were pinned behind my ears. Then she placed the veil on my head, and I looked to my mom with the most heartfelt smile.

I waited until the last possible minute to wiggle into my dress. I faced the full-length mirror as I primped and prepped. A little more lipstick. A few more pokes at my hair. My makeup was soft and natural, except for my vibrant red lips. Then everyone left except my mom. She bunched up the trail, and I gently lifted the front of my dress with two fingers.

At the base of the hill, my vision began to blur. "Should we start walking?" I asked impatiently.

"Let's wait," my brother said.

At first, no one could see me through the line of trees, but a few more steps and then everyone turned to look at me. It was difficult not to rush the walk. I couldn't wait any longer. At the same time, I wanted the moment to last forever. My brother's arm kept me from wobbling. *Rivers Flow in You* played on the harp. And the downpour of rain we were all expecting never came.

The bottom of my dress caught on a few of the rocks, but I wasn't fazed. I could see James. My eyes twinkled, my forehead crinkled, and my face overflowed.

> *I, James, take you, Kara, as a gift from God*
> *And I praise God for your love,*
> *Recognizing that it comes from Him*
> *Whatever happens, through sickness*
> *Health, happiness, sorrow, joy, and pain*
> *I will always be by your side*

Providing for you as a steward of God's creation
I will listen to the truth of God
And lead our family through
Continual prayer for His will
And thanksgiving towards Him
I will trust, respect, help, and care for you
As we walk home to the Lord together
It is my desire to help you become all you were created to be
I will love you faithfully and constantly, now and forever

I, Kara, take you, James, as a gift from God
And I praise God for your love
Recognizing that it comes from Him
Whatever happens, through sickness
Health, happiness, sorrow, joy, and pain
I will always be by your side
Encouraging you as my provider appointed by God
I will listen to the truth of God
And follow your leadership
I will always pray for you
I will trust, respect, help, and care for you
As we walk home to the Lord together
It is my desire to help you become all you were created to be
I will love you faithfully and constantly, now and forever

Then the day was gone. A blink. A memory. It was just a day, but it was a day that changed the trajectory of my entire life. I remember crying, knowing that I wasn't just saying yes to James, I was also saying yes to God.

Entrenched

*"Never fear shadows.
They simply mean there's a light shining somewhere nearby."*
– Ruth E. Renkel

A VEIL, A VOW, A kiss, a cake. But a wedding was only the beginning. Words like "process," "progress," "optimism," "cynicism," "time," and "hope" all collide at once within me. We want simple answers, but we have complex problems. We covet a series of steps, but none exist. We crave that pill on a platter, but there isn't one to take.

It hurt to keep healing, but it would've killed to not.

We were married three months when we drove to Wisconsin. With each mile, my heart beat a little bit faster, and the sky grew a little bit darker. What started out as a sunny, lighthearted drive ended in darkness and terror. For the first time in years, I was home…well, not home. I was in the town I grew up in. I was in a bucket of burdens. Among secrets and sorrow.

It was dark without the false comfort of the city lights. Time spent with family revealed just how numb I'd become. I hadn't truly visited the panic and disgust of my past for more than ten years. Why didn't my dad desire to have any sort of relationship with me? Would he ever attempt to hurt me or my mom?

The negative magnetic pole within my heart repelled against the negativity of that town. Every café, restaurant, store, and bar reminded me of another past relationship. The people I bumped into remembered me by whatever boy I was seeing the last time we conversed. I hated being reminded. I'd all but just forgotten what my scars were or how I got them. I'd emerged from a dark basement, one I'd been in for years. I squinted my eyes at the town, the memories.

I remembered when my dad was about to leave for prison. I'd begged my mom to let me visit him. I was eager to share with my dad everything he'd missed. I'd rehearsed the stories I wanted to express: News regarding school and my participation on the swim team were at the top of my list. But the only thing my dad said to me in the short moments following a brief hug was this: "You're so beautiful." He never asked me about anything. He never listened. He only validated my beauty, and so I sat in silence as my mother and my father civilly discussed the logistics of the divorce. I was 13 the last time I saw my father.

I couldn't breathe, so I placed my head between my knees. As in a dream, everything about my childhood house was different but somehow the same. I knew where I was. I recognized the fence we used to take pictures next to on the first day of school. I could see the barn we built in the backyard. The old, blue paddle boat still leaned against the tool shed. How was it still there?

There was a path I used to go back and forth on as a little girl longing to locate my father. With a series of stacked logs midway and gravel that began at the edge of the fence, the windy, mile-long road led first to my grandmother's house and then to my father's business. And through the woods to grandmother's house we go. But on that day, I saw no woods. No trees. No leaves. I couldn't even see the path right in front of me.

James and I drove the mile down to the lake where I spent most of my childhood days. The same dock remained, but barely. The lake seemed smaller than I'd remembered it. I stepped into the marsh. Water trickled into my shoes. A frog jumped. Catching creatures down by the lake liberated me as a little girl.

The lake was my place, the place I always ran to, even when I wasn't supposed. I've heard the story a number of times: When I was two, I followed our dog down to the lake. I probably grabbed her tail and giggled as I toddled, not understanding that I was running away. Or maybe…maybe I knew.

That day, James caught a frog and handed it to me. I was an adult but still a child. I remembered my dad deeply in that moment. I could almost smell his cigarettes. As I placed the frog back into the water, I confronted the reality that my dad was less than a mile from where I was standing. I crossed my arms. It was time to leave.

I returned to that town a week later for a wedding. Conversations with the people that used to know me aggravated me. My old name—my identity—embarrassed me. Speaking with people who still knew my dad, perhaps saw him just the other week, made me mad. How could near strangers know my dad more than I did? I hated casually talking about my father, all the while ignoring my far from casual past.

Some sins cut so deep that if you're not careful, bitterness will fester like cancer that keeps on growing back. The disease can be cut out repeatedly, but if any trace is left behind, a potential exists for the residuals to grow into a massive hindrance. There are many kinds of cancer. Some are painful and some are incurable, but all cancers are destructive. A lack of forgiveness is the worst kind.

I still remember. I somewhat timidly but mostly eagerly

went outside and sat down next to him. With a fleeting "I'm sorry" and a single wandering tear, forced as it was, I forgave him. And as a result, I'd believed for quite some time that I was beyond my past, above it even. I'd moved on.

I'd mourned the death of my father. I kept commemorative candles lit for a few short months after all was exposed, but eventually the fire blew out. I relinquished all hope. He was dead to me. With a heart cold to the world and a mind absent of reality, the pain was so blissfully distant to me. By choosing to care again, I placed myself in what seemed like a defenseless position. In opting to be invested, I opened a door to possible hurt. I started to let myself believe that my dad could be different, that maybe he was different. And maybe that door needed to be opened once more, as an adult, so that I could close it all the way.

Are we ever really inside our comfort zone when we serve God? I forced myself to step outside. I'd disregarded my feelings for so long that when I finally acknowledged them, I cried. Hard. On autopilot, I contacted my dad's parole officer. Why had I let my fear shut off all emotion towards my dad? The parole officer shared with me that my dad was frightened, apprehensive, and didn't know how to respond to my request to be in contact with him.

Meanwhile, I struggled with the risk. What would come of my heart? Both running and forgiving involve resisting the impulses that scream at you to stop. I let a few droplets smear a few of the words. I liked knowing that in some small way, my dad would soon hold onto my hurt. Then I sealed it, knowing that the shadow of my father would soon be cast over my letter to him:

Dear Dad,

You may be wondering why I chose this method of communication. In all honesty, this option is more difficult for me because it is risky. I risk you not reading this at all. But by me not being present, I remove all distractions from your true reaction to this. I'm choosing not to meet you in person because it removes your fear, your apprehension, my fear, and my emotions from the situation entirely. It's not possible for the next few minutes to revolve around the fear of seeing me, an attempt at deceiving me, or even resistance to hearing what I have to say. It is my hope that my absence will bring authenticity to your reaction.

If I met with you in person, it'd revolve more around my feelings and hope than it would around you anyway. If there's anything I've learned from everything I've experience – good and bad – it's that this isn't about me…Would I love the satisfaction of witnessing your reaction? Of course. Would I love to hold onto hope that things could be different? Of course. But this is not about me. This is about my forgiveness that you can freely take. May you find freedom in my forgiveness that ultimately comes from God. Please watch this video. It's a story about a son and a father. I feel it encompasses the level of forgiveness I offer you…

You broke my heart, Dad.

You made me believe that being beautiful is the only thing that matters in life.

You took away my ability to trust. You brought fear to my life. You damaged our family. They are different because of you.

But I love you. Father, I forgive you. You are forgiven.
Love, Kara

Apparently, my dad fidgeted a little before plainly asking, "What does she want from me?" That was it. Then it was over.

My forgiveness was never about reconciliation or my dad repenting. It was about letting go. How was I no longer angry? How was I able to truly forgive him? I don't know. I guess that's grace. I guess that's God.

I shared the forgiveness letter with my brother, and we started talking on the phone. "Remember when we were kids? Remember the forts we used to build?" The letter led to some of the deepest joy. I was able to reconnect with my brother. It was no longer about my dad not being at my wedding. The point was: My brother was.

Between my focus on my father, fear of my father, and my identity being found in my father, I worshiped him for a long time. I worshiped his thoughts of me. I worshiped his words to me. I worshiped the idea of him coming back to me. I even worshiped the pain that he caused me. But I couldn't continue to worship a relationship with my father (that I never truly had) or the effects of what was done to me. I still pray for my dad, but he may choose to reject God for the rest of his life. I don't want that. I don't understand. And I don't know what will happen. And that's okay.

True healing started with forgiving my dad and releasing myself from the burden of "saving him," but it didn't end there. At one point, it was all a simple equation to me: An acknowledgement of the past sprinkled with a bit of forgiveness, and there you have it: freedom. But then I started to think about the effects and all the lies that had propagated over the years. In *Rid of My Disgrace*, Lindsay and Justine Holcomb present the possible effects of sexual abuse like this:

Sexual assault causes harmful emotional, psychological, and/or physiological effects that are more severe than the effects of other crimes. These effects include: shame, self-blame, guilt, embarrassment, anxiety, stress, fear, anger, confusion, sexualized behaviors, loss of sex drive, interpersonal problems, denial, irritability, depression, despair, social withdrawal, numbing/apathy (detachment, loss of caring), chronic and acute somatizing (experiencing of physical symptoms in response to emotional distress), feelings of isolation and alienation, restricted affect (reduced ability to express emotions), nightmares, flashbacks, headaches, difficulty concentrating, diminished interest in regular activities, negative self-image, loss of self-esteem, emotional shock or numbness, erratic mood swings, feeling powerless, disorientation, OCD, panic attacks, body memories, loss of security, confusion with sex and love, extreme dependency, impaired ability to judge the trustworthiness of others, various phobias, hostility, aggression, change in appetite, suicidal ideation (thoughts of suicide and death), hyper vigilance (always being "on your guard"), insomnia or other sleep disturbance, decreased energy and motivation, exaggerated startle response (jumpiness), eating problems/disorders, self-mutilation (cutting, burning, or otherwise hurting oneself), sexual dysfunction (not being able to perform sexual acts), sexual effects (ranging from avoidance to compulsive promiscuity), hyper arousal (exaggerated feelings or responses to stimuli), inability to concentrate or focus, feeling uncomfortable being alone, gastrointestinal disturbance, substance use and abuse (alcohol and other drugs) and other compulsive behaviors, shock, impaired memory, and post-traumatic stress disorder (PTSD).[9]

The passage reads like the tail end of a drug commercial, when the narrator lists all the potential side effects in three seconds while flowery music drowns out the harshness. That's 60 possible consequences right there. Can you imagine spending nearly 20 years of your life completely unaware that you're experiencing any number of these terrors at the same time? Maybe you can.

On a couch in a therapist's office for the first time in ten years. Nervous. Hesitant. She began labeling me, the little list of words like plastic wrap over my mouth: rumination, obsession, depression, anxiety, post-traumatic stress disorder...The night after my first appointment, I went to an open mic event at a local café and saw a little girl sing and play her guitar. She had to be, what, 12? She seemed so innocent, and in that moment, I realized that I never got to be her, but I could've been her. She was me, just without the burden of my dad. In *Secret Survivors*, Blume illustrates this grieving process:

> *Bereavement theory is necessary to address the other aspect of family trauma: the emotional loss suffered by the child. The abused child has much to mourn. She grieves the loss of the family she would have wanted, and the safe, warm love that a family is supposed to represent. She grieves lost hopes, lost safety, lost innocence. She grieves her childhood. And she grieves the view of the world as a safe place, for that is lost to her forever.*[10]

The truth was, I'd been grieving for years, I just didn't know it. And in my most grief-stricken moments, I rebelled and allowed the initial shame of what was done to me to wash over me. As a teenager enslaved to my worth, I passively complied. My past was "gone" because I wasn't consciously thinking about it anymore.

Around this same time, I made a list of the names and the associated hurt. I prayed and one by one I released them. Each tear represented a single regret. There were many. Then I lit the piece of paper on fire. The ashes were scars, remnants of the sin that would remain but surely fade. It was the sweetest form of revenge, to let go. To not be hurt by them anymore.

I'd stepped into a world I had no idea existed. I was doing a lot of work with my past, but that work brought me to a desperate place. Belief in God and not having the guts to execute what I thought about doing to myself—that's what was keeping me alive. Receiving that diagnosis didn't exactly help me. I found it to be harsh and hardly hopeful. I questioned if anyone really cared for me. I took the prescription, along with its message: Something was terribly wrong with me. I was quiet, barely breathing.

I hunched over on my bed, my legs folded like a pretzel, my head tilted down. With each blink, a tear plopped down onto the sheets. They didn't fall down my cheeks. They just dropped. I was silent. I didn't sob. Sobbing signified hope, but I didn't have any. The thoughts harassed me. Intruded. Welcoming them was easier, because then there was no struggle.

Would James ever understand? I stared at the picture of myself in the frame on our dinner table. The image was captured when we were engaged. I was stretched out on my stomach as I rested in the long, green grass. My feet were in the air, crossed behind me. My head was tilted to the side, and my hair fell elegantly over my shoulder. My smile expanded so wide that my eyes were hardly open. Had I forgotten about my pain then or was I free from it? The frame of the picture was a mirror. I stared at myself, both who I thought I was then and who I was finding myself to be.

I was disgusted at the thought of faking another smile.

Looking into the eyes of friends was painful. In between half hugs and staring at the ground, resentment creeped in. And when we'd gaze at each other in silence, I could still hear the thoughts.

Eventually, I disclosed my suicidal thoughts, my brokenness, and my weakness. And I'd never felt more loved than when James read Bible verses over me and my friends prayed for me. To be weak in their eyes was horrifying, but I think it actually made me stronger.

The first therapist I met with early on in my marriage was a woman named Robbin, and the irony wasn't lost on me. She was a pastor's wife. Around 50, with light blonde hair that was slowly fading to grey. Always had a dress on. She reminded me of a detective. During our third session, I told Robbin about my trip to Wisconsin.

"Okay, relax. Take a deep breath," she interrupted me mid-sentence. I *hated* when people would tell me to relax, as if it was something I had control over.

"I've been to my hometown twice this month. James and I argue a lot. I guess I've thought about harming myself. And when I needed someone the most, no one showed up," I shared.

She told me it was too much to handle. Asked how the medications were working. I told her how James felt hurt by how vigilant I was around him. I was always watching to make sure he wasn't looking at other women.

And she told me that men are created to be more sexual than women, that God designed it to be that way, that I couldn't expect James to control himself. "You need to understand this. You need to accept this," she concluded. "If I had to guess, I'd say he's having sexual thoughts, but he's ashamed of them. He wants to please you. That's why he doesn't tell you about these thoughts." Robbin was the worst person I could've been talking to right then.

We argued until I stopped defending the truth because I fully believed the lie. I walked away from that woman convinced that James would never have eyes for just me. And that's when the thoughts of hurting myself got bad, real bad. Fortunately, James came home before anything happened.

According to 2 Chronicles 32:1, we can be faithful to God and be centered in His will for us and still be attacked. In my first six attempts at therapy, I encountered individuals who were quick to diagnose, eager to medicate, hesitant to care, and slow to offer true Biblical advice. Medication could've helped, but it didn't because there wasn't any action prescribed to go along with it. And no one reminded me to have hope. No one prayed for me. No one helped me come up with strategies to address the mindsets, the habits, and my past.

When I received that diagnosis, I began to play the part of a depressed, anxious, jumpy, helpless victim. No doctor ventured to identify me as a survivor. I was simply seen as a casualty of war, one to take pity upon. I'm not disputing medicine or therapy by any means, but maybe I never needed someone to recite a list of mental illnesses to me, at least not in that way. I could attest to my wounded state of mind and marred heart prior to ever stepping foot into any doctor's office.

Encouraged

*"Life can only be understood backwards;
but it must be lived forwards."*
– Søren Kierkegaard

I'D WON MANY BATTLES, BUT a war raged on. And as I began to peel back the layers, I saw that I'd been merely finding "more acceptable" ways to earn my worth. Instead of sleeping around, I was aiming for a Boston Marathon qualifying time. I was working hard at being skinny. Crazy. Anything else to define me. I loved being a runner instead of an abuse victim. I loved being considered crazy instead of a victim, skinny instead of a victim, *anything* instead of a victim. Another accomplishment was another label to drown out my past. Vain hope that a new label could take over and define me.

I thought I had it all figured out. I'd formulated a long list of everything in my life that needed to change. I spent far too much time in front of the mirror. I cared too much about what others believed about me, especially men. And I didn't trust anyone.

The tip of my iceberg was everything I could see, hear, and feel: The pain, the lies, and the emptiness. The bulk of that big block of ice was everything else: My past, how my past affected my present, and my beliefs. Straining to address only the symptoms was like trying to shovel the ocean. I worked hard, but nothing really changed. Beliefs give rise to values and values give rise to desires. Desires gives rise to actions. In the same way, at the bottom of every bad behavior lived a lie. And the farther I traveled down that iceberg, the darker it became.

Each fear and unfortunate experience forced the faucet knob to turn further, allowing additional lies to pour forth. They built on each other and gained momentum until there was a rapid rush of water, a current of lies. Other times, the faucet only leaked. The problem had nothing to do with the knob but everything to do with the wellbeing of source, the faucet itself, myself. The worst was the annoying drip, drip, drip of a leaky faucet, my constant tendency to believe the lie.

Without a radiant and perfect God emitting light, I never would've been able to grasp what truly existed within my iceberg, especially at the bottom. Did you know that black, inch-long worms dwell within them? They're rare creatures that live inside this large chunk of ice. It's not known how ice worms can tunnel their way through the ice, but they can make their way through every part of it. And like these worms, the lies can make their way through our lives, infecting our beliefs and attacking our desires and values.

Ice worms can't survive in temperatures above freezing. The warmth kills them. Under warm light the worms liquefy. Likewise, our lies turn to goo in the presence of light. They're still there, but much like the worms, once the lies encounter warm light, they don't stand much of a chance.

Without awareness, nothing can be changed. Awareness has one primary goal, and that is to make the implicit, explicit. Identifying why I thought the way that I did was key. I asked why until I couldn't ask it anymore, and this is what I found: I'd believed I was just a body, one that would never please anyone. Because I didn't believe that God could truly love someone like me.

Healing is complicated. Plural. Ongoing. But as complex as healing is, most of it can be wrapped up in a single word: Identity.

Jesus saves me, clothes me, and is healing me instead of giving me what I deserve. Within this grace is the power to change. Within this love is the power to redefine true beauty. One day, Jesus will tell me just how beautiful I truly am, not because of the body that's been given to me or the story that's been handed to me, but because of the beauty I have in Him.

The ugliest part about me wasn't me. It was my insecurity. My inability to see myself as beautiful. The ugliest part about me was my inability to believe God when He told me that He loved me. How about a math analogy: Take the limit of my insecurity as God's love approached infinity, and all my insecurity should've blown away.

Insecurity is a mind-consuming, joy-squishing form of anxiety. It's uncomfortable and undeniably a sort of curse. It can transform every thought into something impure, something evil. I remembered my dad identifying me as fat, my doctor labeling me as overweight, and my dates professing the perfection of pornography. I remembered it all the time, and it wasn't until I'd been married for a couple of years that I began to wonder if my life could be any different. John Eldredge puts it this way:

> *Something awful has happened; something terrible. Something worse, even, than the fall of man. For in that greatest of all tragedies, we merely lost Paradise — and with it, everything that made life worth living. What has happened since is unthinkable: we've gotten used to it. We're broken in to the idea that this is just the way things are. The people who walk in great darkness have adjusted their eyes.*[8]

Normal. Sometimes it's conforming to the world around you. Sometimes it's what everybody else thinks you should be. Other times normal can be thought of as something that's only defined by you. Normal is something you've spent your whole life living. Normal is your expected, your typical.

But what if "normal" had the potential to be something far greater than I'd ever dreamed it could be? Was it actually possible to *truly* overcome all that was lost? These are the questions that led me to try Eye Movement Desensitization and Reprocessing (EMDR) therapy. EMDR was the biggest game changer when it came to tools that aided in my healing as an adult.

I pressed on with therapy because my past obviously still affected me. I felt like an outsider, like I was lesser than everyone else. I was annoyed with my fear of the dark. I didn't believe James when he told me that I was beautiful or when he told me that he loved me. Intimacy was difficult. I didn't connect emotionally during sex. I wanted — we needed — my life to be different.

In EMDR, I learned that a certain part of my brain is my storehouse for a web of sorts. We'll call this location my Trauma Holder. In this web was a series of emotional memories. They were intricately entwined, so much so that the recollection of one led to a recollection of a whole bunch of them. Perhaps I didn't recall them in the fundamental sense. I wasn't seeing flashes of the memories. Instead, I remembered them in my emotions and in my body.

There's another part of my brain where other types of memories are stored. Let's call this place my Safe Place. It's a place where I remember trivial, unemotional things like what I wore to work yesterday. These memories are facts. It isn't that my other memories aren't also facts. They are. But my other memories, the traumatic ones, were all tangled together. And they carried with them unpleasant things like lies and fear and shame and depression and anxiety.

EMDR was the process of teasing out my traumatic memories from my Trauma Holder one by one and placing them into my Safe Place. I still remember everything that's ever happened to me, but now I can recall all that has happened without simultaneously reliving the fear, shame, and intense "differentness."

During EMDR therapy, I held a vibration device in each hand. Back and forth and back and forth. It simulated what happens during the REM cycle of sleep, when significant restoration and processing take place. The REM stage of sleep is when the mind attempts to make sense of all the previous day's happenings.

We processed the abuse, relationships, the newspaper article, even getting robbed in Honduras. I used to run to my garage in the morning because of how terrified I was of the dark. My heart would race in full-blown panic. I had no idea that that kind of hypervigilance wasn't normal, that therapy could take that away. Through EMDR, I went from unsure to bold. I also realized that I don't need to be in pain to be loved. I think a part of me had held on to the suffering because of the attention and the "love" it provided me.

Through EMDR, I became more joyful. I had more energy again. I learned to have compassion for my child self. Through EMDR, I believe I returned to myself.

I'm still a human with a past though. The therapy hasn't made me immune to the memories or to feeling sad because of them. Scattered and searing. Fragmented and falling. Of all things, the song *Feliz Navidad* really tripped me up one year. Alone. In the car. Listening. It brought me back:

I was in the back seat. My dad was in the front. The radio on, the snow falling, the tree on top.

The tree on top.

And my dad…being Dad. He was goofy and silly and somewhat happy, even if it was a lie. We blasted that song that day. And I wouldn't have had it any other way. Part of healing was learning to accept the positive memories too. And learning to be present in the emotions, not be afraid of them, and know that they wouldn't kill me.

It was in darkness that I walked the path to my dad's house in the dead of winter. It was in darkness that I slept in my abandoned, empty, childhood home in post-promiscuity shame. It was in darkness that I sat hunched over, unable to breathe. It was in darkness that my mom drove me to the pet store to purchase an aquarium in attempt to bring even the tiniest bit of light into my life. It was in darkness that I witnessed the death of those fish, the death of my childhood, the death of me.

But it's over. A big part of my healing has been letting go of the "never over." It can be over. It *is* over.

I will always remember my dad, but I'm free from bondage to a name. I will think of him and wonder, *what is he doing right now?* I will remember the darkness. But I'll also remember that henceforth, the darkness will only decrease.

I've also had to learn how to be okay with my body, in my body. As an adult, I've outgrown the chubbiness. But being skinny and feeling pretty delivers a false sense of security. It actually bothers me when other women look at me and see this beautiful, thin woman. Because I *know*. A lot of times, women roll their eyes at me as if I know nothing about the dieting world or feeling ugly or feeling like a foreigner in my own body. I want women to look past the exterior and see that no matter what she looks like, she too has probably warred with weight, beauty, and insecurity.

I don't think it's wrong to want to be beautiful, but a healed, healthy outlook on beauty has meant that I've had to learn to let go of comparison, stop weighing myself all the time, and release all expectations around my appearance when it comes to aging and changing. I don't watch much TV. I'm very selective when it comes to the movies I'll go see. I don't read many magazines. No, I can't escape the world, but I can ignore parts of it. Doing so makes it a lot easier to win the fights and engage in the war.

Much of my healing has also been wrapped up in my marriage. There have been times when I've been afraid to have children or to grow another year older because I've feared to lose that "security." But with every passing year, with each child, with all my changes, in every new environment, I gain another data point of love that swings me back around to the truth. Healing has been largely about collecting data points that refute my past. And through James, I have a lot of data points. I have a better, unperfect understanding of the love of God.

Because if God is love, and I am one with God because of Christ, then love floods through my veins. God not only loves me; the love of God also resides in me. If God is love, then God is patient with me. He is kind and not jealous in a worldly sense. He's not boastful, proud, or rude. God doesn't demand His own way, but rather, He waits for me to choose Him. He keeps no record of my wrongs—the ways in which I've personally wronged Him through my insecurity.

God rejoices when truth wins. He never gives up on me and never loses faith in me. He is always hopeful. Most of all, the love of God endures through every circumstance. God is love. He is a love I couldn't escape from even if I tried. I am God's creation, and to recognize this identity is to live in security. James has shown me a lot of this truth in an incredibly amazing, terribly unperfect way.

Loved

My finger moves up and down the center of his chest.
My eyes follow the traces.
I see all my torn-up places.
So I excuse myself from connecting with his eyes.
But my heart isn't absent of the desire to gaze into them.
Rather, it's fear that prevents me from seeing him.
Eventually I succumb.
I do all that I can to rid myself of the feeling of numb.
I allow the magnetic pull to draw my forehead closer to his.
I lift my lids.
I wince as I would at the sight of the sun
Because his eyes remind me of what can't be undone.
Proverbial.
His eyes are so familiar.
When we finally lock, I see more than I'd hoped for.
Like my own and my father's, his eyes I adore.
They are dark and brown and soft yet serious.
And for a moment, they are my father's distant eyes.
And they mirror back to me.
These windows tell me who I am.
They scream to me where I've been.
His eyes.
Like a fake form of nostalgia, I long for the love that was never there.
A better time of the past that never existed.
I've wanted love, but it seems that I've missed it.
His eyes help me to realize, maybe what was numb can be undone.

Never have I believed the words, "I love you."
So I sigh and I cry. I cry and I sigh.
I try to cup my hands around what cannot be seen.
I attempt to hold onto this newly acknowledged dream.
"You really love me?" I say.
"Yes," he says.
"I loved you then. And I still love you today."

I'd prayed that God would give me a little girl, but He knew that giving me a boy a first would bring about even more healing. In motherhood I've found healing. I love seeing that my body can have another, incredibly beautiful, non-sexual purpose. I melt at the sound of my son singing to me at night, "Rock a bye Mommy on the tree top…"

Loving my husband and my son helps me to hold onto the hope that men can be different, that they are different. Some bits of healing were even smaller than baby steps, little breaths of air, littler reminders of what is true, like when I was interviewed for this book and when I shared a condensed version of this story with a bunch of men at a church gathering. Those men are different. Data point after data point, spinning, swinging, twirling around the truth.

People like to ask me if it's difficult for me to talk about my past. I'm actually a little disturbed by how normal it's become. But I guess anything can become "normal" if you do it long enough. And honestly, being open about it strips my past of its power over me.

I like to think of it like this: We begin our lives as little tadpoles—children with complete trust in God in the water. We assume without questioning that our Father's will is just and holy and perfect. Eventually we evolve into adults. We become comfortable on land, and begin to follow whatever we see fit. Suddenly, living in the water isn't the most natural thing anymore, yet we were born in that water—we were made in the image of God. I was created in the image of God. I must remember that I can still swim. I can still have faith like the child I once was but never truly got to be. I can still trust just as blindly as I used to without carrying with me the burden of what was done to me.

As I accept my past, embrace my present, and plan for our family's future, I realize that I am grounded, maybe for the first time ever. A single piece of driftwood lost at sea, the current working to bring me back to God, to myself, to life. Where sin abounds, grace abounds all the more. My life was destined to endless change—the traveling and continual motion of one season transforming to the next—to beg me to *become* the change. The revolution called My Life was always meant to arouse the uprising within me. Vulnerability is not a weakness. My vulnerability is healing me.

I was able to finally rebel against my own humanity, to begin to leave the sinful complexions of myself and those around me and hold fast to the Spirit of God within me. To not only let go of my dad, but to also forgive myself.

My dad was intended to be shadow that would point to a much greater reality, but like many others, he hasn't fulfilled his role. The shadow that my father cast over my life darkened my sight and tarnished my heart, but the shadow of God the Father is unchanging and protecting. His shadow is vastly different from the evil shadows of this world. I had never known God as a father. Because I already had a father and he meant everything to me. But the more I could let go of my earthly father, the more I could grab onto God.

After his brothers disowned him and left him for dead, Joseph forgave them. Joseph chose to see a purpose for his pain. He said, "You intended to harm me, but God intended it for good to accomplish what is now being done, the saving of many lives" (Genesis 50:20). I love this because I do think that God is using my story for good. I honestly can't imagine my life without tragedy. What if all that's transpired is all that ever could've brought me to right here? Right now. Where I continue to come to the end of myself, where my only option is to turn to God. And at the intersection of fury and gratitude I find the most peculiar thing. I find exhilaration. And hope.

Notes

[1] Moore, Beth. *Beloved Disciple: The Life and Ministry of John,* Living Proof Ministries, 2002.

[2] Excerpt from *I Dreamed a Dream*, lyrics from the original French musical Les Misérables by Alain Boublil (translated into English by Herbert Kretzmer).

[3] *A Profile of Pedophilia: Definition, Characteristics of Offenders, Recidivism, Treatment Outcomes, and Forensic Issues*, Mayo Clinic Proceedings, Volume 82, Issue 4, 457:471, April 2007, <http://www.mayoclinicproceedings.org>.

[4] *Sex Addiction*, Sexual Conditions Health Center, WebMD, LLC, 2012, <http://www.webmd.com>.

[5] Merriam-Webster, 2012, "Manipulation."

[6] Stout. Martha, *The Sociopath Next Door*, Broadway Books, 2005, 1.

[7] Herman, Judith. Father-Daughter Incest, by the President and Fellows of Harvard College, 2003, 118.

[8] Eldredge, John. *The Journey of Desire*, Thomas Nelson, Inc., 2000.

[9] Holcomb, Justin S. and L.A. *Rid of My Disgrace*, Wheaton, Illinois: Crossway, 2011, 39:44.

[10] Blume, E. Sue. *Secret Survivors: Uncovering Incest and Its Aftereffects in Women*, The Random House Publishing Group, 1990, 50:79.

www.ingramcontent.com/pod-product-compliance
Lightning Source LLC
Chambersburg PA
CBHW070549050426
42450CB00011B/2783